Twiceborn

BOOKS
IRH PRESS
New York

ISBN 13: 978-1-942125-74-7
ISBN 10: 1-942125-74-7

Printed in Canada

First Edition

Twiceborn

My Early Thoughts that Revealed
My True Mission

RYUHO
OKAWA

IRH Press

At around the age of two

During Kawashima Junior High School days
in Tokushima Prefecture

At the New York Headquarters of a Japanese trading house

During Jonan High School days
At his birth home in Kawashima Town, Tokushima Prefecture, Japan

Contents

PART ONE

El Cantare in Youth

CHAPTER ONE

Starting from the Ordinary

CHAPTER TWO

The Spirit of Being Independent

CHAPTER FIVE

Existence and Time

CHAPTER SIX

To the Extraordinary Heights of Love

PART TWO
The Victory of Faith

Preface to the New Edition

The former edition of this book was published on my 32nd birthday, under the title *Starting from the Ordinary*. It was only two years after I founded Happy Science. I wrote this semi-autobiographical book as I successively put out many books on spiritual messages like a great torrent of Light. Despite my hard work, the days felt too short; I had a long way to go before I could achieve my goal.

Three years later, on March 7, 1991, Happy Science was officially recognized as a religious organization in Japan, and in July of the same year, we held our first Celebration of the Lord's Descent at Tokyo Dome. It was in that lecture that I declared myself to be El Cantare.* This event made the name Ryuho Okawa and the existence of Happy Science become widely known throughout Japan.

This provided me with proof of success, but at the same time, it marked the beginning of a battle against numerous mass media organizations. Some critics said that I was just an upstart who had started from "the ordinary" and that such success was unacceptable. It was groundless criticism from people who had a shallow understanding of my book, *Starting from the Ordinary*.

I remember being called a genius on many occasions from about the age of two into my 20s. As I grew older, more people described me as such. Nevertheless, I thought that being easily satisfied with other people praising me for my talents would lead me to corruption, so I decided to make it a principle to find joy in making efforts.

---

*Translator's Footnote: Okawa's very first lecture in Tokyo Dome is compiled in Part Two of this book.

Many Buddhist scriptures refer to Gautama Siddhartha in his early days as a bodhisattva—someone undergoing spiritual discipline to attain enlightenment. Eventually, he attained Great Enlightenment and became Buddha, the Grand Master. He called himself Buddha, meaning "Enlightened One." But this was not out of conceit; it was because he believed it to be true. And so, the Great Tathagata was born.

However, many of his disciples in later generations devoted themselves to religious training as monks and nuns in admiration of Gautama the bodhisattva. I believe that describing my life before I attained Great Enlightenment will also be a gift for future generations.

I dedicate *El Cantare in Youth* to all the bodhisattvas who are yet to come.

It is all right to be ordinary; just continue your spiritual discipline.

Ryuho Okawa
Master and CEO of Happy Science Group
July 7, 2002 (my 46th birthday)

Preface to the Original Edition

Until now, I have avoided any references to my personal life as much as possible, focusing solely on publishing the Laws, or the Truth. This is because, in the words of an ancient proverb, "He who would go a hundred miles should consider ninety-nine as halfway." I always tell myself that I should never be satisfied with small successes if I am to go beyond "a thousand miles."

A biography certainly touches the hearts of many, but if you become intoxicated with your own experiences, your philosophical development will cease. Although this book contains some semi-autobiographical memories, its purpose is to reveal the origins of my thoughts and the process by which my philosophy of Truth was formed.

It is my hope that this book will serve as a key to understanding the vast system of Truth taught at Happy Science. I also pray it will be a guidepost of life for young people who are walking on the path to enlightenment and those who have yet to come.

Ryuho Okawa
Master and CEO of Happy Science Group
July 7, 1988 (my 32nd birthday)

Translator's Note: The two prefaces were given for Part One, "El Cantare in Youth."

PART ONE

El Cantare in Youth

CHAPTER ONE

Starting from the Ordinary

1

The Awareness of Being Ordinary

I have decided to publish *El Cantare in Youth—Starting from the Ordinary*. Let me start by touching upon the reasons why I decided to write a book with such a title. As a matter of fact, I myself was quite an ordinary person from the outset. Although I started out as an average person, I eventually came to teach others and write numerous books, thereby enlightening people of the world. Looking back over my past endeavors, I feel I have developed a mindset or way of thinking that deserves to be made public.

I believe the very phrase "starting from the ordinary" is words of enlightenment. Most people seem to drift in everyday laziness without reflecting deeply on themselves, and unknowingly lose sight of themselves. On the other hand, people who are aware of their mediocrity seem to be acutely conscious of the problems at hand. Such awareness will allow them to recognize the limits of their ability and strength, and lead them to make efforts to somehow overcome them with new ideas and ingenuity.

I was probably around 10 years old when I first recognized that I was mediocre. In those days, I felt keenly that I was an ordinary person in terms of my ability, physical strength, and looks. But even though I was ordinary in every respect, at least I wanted to maintain high hopes for the future. So, I would always hold my ideals high. It was a tremendous challenge for me to figure out how to achieve these ideals and go on to attain an extraordinary state because I knew I was an ordinary person.

I believe recognizing one's mediocrity is an important starting point when setting out on a long journey to achieve extraordinary heights. In fact, recognizing your mediocrity means knowing all your strong and weak points through careful observation. Only after thoroughly examining all of your strengths and weaknesses will you be able to understand the extent of your potential.

Around the time I became aware of my mediocrity, I had two dreams. My first dream was to become a scholar; I wished to put my ideas out into the world and teach people. My second dream was to become a diplomat; I wished to work across international borders, interact with people from different countries, and broaden my capacity as a human being. Between the ages of 10 and 12, these two ideals grew in my heart.

Many years have passed since then, and I am now the CEO of Happy Science. I did not become a scholar, but my job involves writing books and teaching people from a podium. In this respect, I could say my first dream has nearly come true.

Moreover, before I entered the path of Truth, I spent about six years at a Japanese trading house and worked at the leading edge of international business. Being involved in matters of the international economy, I always kept an eye on developments in Japan and abroad. I learned about the current global situations every day and undertook a variety of tasks in that work environment. Although I was not exactly a diplomat, I could say I worked as a diplomat of the private sector.

In this way, I have achieved both of my dreams to some extent, though in a somewhat different framework than I had expected. As Happy Science expands its activities from Japan to other countries, I hope my first and second dreams will come together to produce even greater fruits.

In this book, I want to share with you the essence of what I thought and learned as a young man. It will reveal what made me decide to launch an organization that would promote the study, exploration, and spreading of the Truth, and why I passionately continue to advance this movement even now. I can see the lights of Truth shining brilliantly in my personal experiences, which I believe will serve as guideposts of hope for many people as well.

2

Like a Turtle

Looking back at my childhood, I feel keenly that I was advancing through life like a turtle. Born in the countryside of Shikoku Island, I was brought up as an ordinary child. I completed my elementary and secondary education in ordinary local schools, and I eventually developed my self-awareness.

My parents were pure at heart and hardworking. They never told me to study. Rather, I had a natural urge to seriously study many different things, one after another.

When I was around eight years old and in the second grade, my father took me to a neighboring town to buy me a big study desk. We visited a shop full of wooden furniture where my father bought me a desk and said, "This is going to be your desk, son." I still remember how excited I was. To a primary school student, the desk looked very large and its wood grains were so vivid. I looked forward to studying at the desk when I got a little bigger.

When I was about 10 and reached the fourth grade, I started to use the desk to study. At that time, we owned a secondary house about 200 meters (218 yards) away from our main house, and I would go there to study. It was a special feeling; I felt like I was given my own castle upon reaching the upper grades of primary school.

Every night after dinner, I would pick up my bag and walk down the dark street to the secondary house. Then, I would go upstairs, turn on the light bulb, and enter my study room.

Since I was still young at the time, I was very scared of the dark. It was indeed frightening to leave my parents to walk to the site. It was not a sturdy concrete building or a new wooden house, but a very old wooden structure that had once been a factory; it was so old that a draft would blow through the cracks, and plaster would fall off the walls here and there.

I would shut myself in, turn on the bare 60-watt bulb, and study. It was an amazing feeling indeed. Sitting in that old wooden building made me feel like one of the heroes from the adventure stories I read when I was very little, such as *The Adventures of Tom Sawyer*.

Every day, I would study and ponder various things alone in that place. I believe it served as the basis for my ability to think deeply and contemplate in later years. At the age of 10, I was already developing the habit of thinking for myself.

The building was very old, and the cold wind would come in through the cracks in the winter. There was no heating, so I would always wrap an old threadbare blanket around my waist and wear gloves to study. It was so cold that I would also wear a thick jacket, a warm hat, and a face mask to cover my mouth. In the beginning, I wore thick leather gloves, but since it was difficult to write with a pencil, I switched to thin, silk gloves instead. But they were not warm enough to protect my hands from the cold; my fingers were always numb and blue.

So, that became my habit; I would shut myself in the secondary house almost every night and study or contemplate various things by myself until about midnight.

In those times, I did not use an efficient method to study. For example, when I studied social studies, like world geography or history, I would copy the entire contents of the textbooks into my notebooks instead of reading just the important points. Compared to the studying techniques I learned later, this was an extremely simple way of studying. At the ages of 10 and 11, I spent night after night copying the textbooks and felt as if I were copying sutras or something holy. I now feel quite nostalgic about how I studied in such a simplistic way.

I still could not tell which way I should be heading, but I truly loved the feeling of making efforts to achieve something lofty, something sublime. Even today, I can vividly remember the feeling I had at the time. It was around then that I began to seriously appreciate the spirit of conquering the weak self. Despite using such an inefficient method to study, my performance at school gradually improved.

I had a brother who was four years older than I. He was rather precocious. Even in kindergarten and the early years of primary school, he displayed great intellect, and my parents had high hopes for him in his future. He always studied his lessons ahead of time, whereas I concentrated on revision. Compared to my brother, I felt I was really slow at producing results. At the time, I was still unaware of the importance of learning in depth and was only concerned about the speed at which my studies progressed.

In those days, there was always a thought in my mind that said, "I'm an ordinary person and not particularly clever. But even though I'm not so clever, if I spend three or four hours doing what other people cover in an hour, I may be able to catch up to them. If I persevere four or five years doing what other people tire of after one year, I may certainly be able to master the subject. Although I am aware of being ordinary, if I give five, 10, or 20 years of continued effort, it will most probably bring about a new change. My intellect may be average, but if I work to build up my store of knowledge and persevere, surely I can one day make a huge leap, like a chemical reaction taking place."

With such a hope in mind, I would hold my pencil tight and breathe on my white silk gloves to warm my fingers. My aunt, who was a novelist, commented that I was a man of effort, and this encouraged me greatly in those days.

3

Essential Daily Attitudes

In my boyhood, I always kept one idea in my mind, which was, "No matter how remote or small the location or community in which one resides may be, those who start to shine under those circumstances can never know how much light they might actually possess." My father would often remind me of this as well.

I usually ranked first in class, and on seeing this, my father said, "No matter how remotely the school may be located or how small it is, the top student is always special. Even when compared to everyone else in the whole country, that student might be on another level. Unlike those who rank second or below, there is no way of knowing how much the top student is capable of; the student could be a great genius. No matter how rural the area, how small the school, or how limited the community may be, the person at the top may possess incomparable value." He always encouraged me in this way. As I recall, those words supported me greatly.

Looking back from where I stand now, there is not a big difference whether one comes in first or second, but I learned an important lesson at the time: "No matter how small a place may be or what region or position one may be in, someone who emits extraordinary light in a given situation may find that they actually possess surprisingly great value."

As I grew up, I gradually understood just how true these words were. No matter what kind of environment you find yourself in, if you shine like a diamond in your current situation, you will eventually find that a new path, or a new life, will open for you. I have come to know this to be true.

Since I experienced this myself, when I later had people working for me, I was able to take a fresh approach with them. I naturally came to think, "I am in this position now because other people recognized my potential at some point. So, I also want to search for talented people who deserve similar assistance. I want to seek out wonderful people and lift them from sluggish mediocrity to extraordinary heights."

Those who are aware of their mediocrity should keep in mind the following three attitudes on a daily basis. The first is to always remember to make efforts. If you are aware of your mediocrity and want to rise above it, you need to keep making efforts. It is extremely important to encourage yourself and live with a spirit of conquering the weak self.

I still have an image of the Yoshino River, otherwise known as "Shikoku Saburo," which flows through the hills and plains of Shikoku Island. It starts as a small stream in the mountains, but it grows into a wide, majestic river as it flows downstream. This river holds many of my childhood memories. I used to play on its banks when I was very small. I can still see the shining silver reflections on the river. Just like the flow of this river, I am sure our lives will eventually widen, deepen, and flow gracefully as we continue making efforts. This is essential in leading a successful life.

The second important attitude is to have ideals. No matter how small an insect may be, it will not die easily if it has something to live for. It will hang on to life tenaciously. Some insects fly off to look for light. They fly in constant search of an everlasting light. If even insects make efforts to fly in search of light, how meaningless would it be for humans to live without ideals? Have you ever considered this?

I have seen many people who, despite having ideals in their youth, eventually let their dreams wither and die. Many seem to have lost their ideals especially after entering university. I have also seen those who gradually lost their ideals and gave in to reality within a year or two after starting work.

However, you must not allow your ideals to be simply swept away. If you recognize your mediocrity and your starting point as an ordinary person, you must always hold your ideals high, even if others laugh at you or call you incompetent. I have come to realize that living with ideals is the driving force that will ultimately help you achieve great self-realization.

People sometimes consider those who hold ideals as too naive. However, endeavors that have truly contributed to the advancement of humanity and changed the course of human history were, in fact, founded on the very actions others regarded as naive. We should never lose this naivete.

The third important attitude is to build up tangible results daily. Please know that it is impossible for an ordinary person to reach great heights in just one leap. There are certainly people who suddenly become stars, great poets, or famous authors overnight, but we know that their success does not generally last long. I have seen many people who seemed to attain popularity for a certain period of time or due to some chance event, but eventually they sank into oblivion. Such successes cannot possibly be true ones.

Therefore, it is important to always remember to build up positive results on a daily basis. Accumulate small, successful experiences little by little, one step at a time. However small a success may be, if you accumulate five or 10 of these, you will gain confidence and eventually find new possibilities opening up before you.

There is nothing more important for someone who has started from the ordinary than to view life and success as a buildup of positive results. Accumulation is essential. Rather than aiming to hit a one-off home run, try to accumulate single hits. I believe this attitude is the most important requirement for achieving success.

4

Discoveries

Having started from the ordinary, life will eventually start to flow greatly. In the process, it is important to make discoveries once in a while.

Life is a series of discoveries. What kinds of discoveries are there? I would say there are two kinds: discoveries within oneself and discoveries outside oneself.

Inner discoveries are extremely significant during adolescence. Everyone goes through a period when they develop their inner self by reading various novels or becoming absorbed in poetry. At such times, we may be surprised to find so many hidden elements in our minds and realize the vastness of the mental space we have inside of ourselves.

In the process of exploring our inner space, we come in contact with other people. We then realize that the self-image we had in our minds can actually be found externally, in the outside world. This is a truly new discovery. We find that we are not the only ones who have worries; others share similar concerns. This is when our views on human beings deepen.

In fact, the kind of person you are and the kind of views you have on life depend on how many discoveries you have made in the course of your life. People do not necessarily take note of every discovery they make, so the number of discoveries one has made remains unknown, but the accumulation of people's daily discoveries is actually manifested in the differences in their characters.

Of course, a person's discoveries may vary according to his or her given circumstances. Those born with robust physical bodies that would enable them to become Olympic athletes will probably have discoveries mainly related to speed, stamina, or athletic skills. But the majority of people are not blessed with the bodies of successful Olympic athletes, so they are more concerned about things that commonly worry people. This, in a sense, is something to be grateful for.

From this, we can say that being born with average physical and intellectual abilities means we can live our lives by sharing many common traits with the majority of people. In fact, this is the way to discover the universal Truth of all humankind within oneself. I am convinced that this universal Truth actually lies dormant in one's awareness of being ordinary.

What is important is the fact that the quality of your discoveries can be deepened in two stages. The first stage is the discovery of the actual state of being—the nature of other people and an understanding of oneself and what lies within. The second stage is a discovery from a completely new perspective. It is to understand oneself, others, and the world from a totally different angle. Such discovery is possible, and I must touch upon this possibility.

You can gain new clues to understand yourself through the words of others or in the form of inspiration that comes from heaven when you practice self-reflection or meditation on your own. Sometimes you can learn about a new aspect of yourself in a completely unexpected way. Likewise, you can sometimes unintentionally learn something new about other people. Even if you may have had difficulty grasping the meaning of the existence or character of others in the past, as you accumulate various experiences, your scope of understanding will expand and it will become easier for you to understand more people and their nature.

Gaining a new understanding of others or finding out what you did not understand before will bring you the joy of discovery, and this is an important aspect of making discoveries. The more things you discover, the richer your life, and therefore your life lessons, will be. This is when the discoveries of an ordinary person come to have a positive effect based on the principle of accumulation.

What is taught in school as knowledge or information is limited, but the learning done in the name of "personal discovery" is unlimited. It has infinite possibilities and contains boundless potential. This is your own personal study. For the ordinary person, this kind of unique, personal study to make discoveries is more important than anything else.

5

New Developments in Life

So far, I have talked about recognizing one's mediocrity, advancing like a turtle, essential daily attitudes, and the importance of accumulating discoveries. I will now talk about new developments in life.

If you wish to achieve a particular ideal in this lifetime, you need to amass all your powers and focus them in a new direction. There is no success without new developments or innovation. This is at least true for ordinary people. Without new developments, neither success nor ideals can be realized.

As you accumulate discoveries and life lessons, you will develop greatness of character. What, then, would you achieve after having built greatness of character? How would you release your energy like a gushing torrent? This is a very difficult challenge and an advanced test in life. It is a question of how to make good use of opportunities.

While you may wish to live a quiet life, it is very rare for people to live their whole lives without undergoing any change; in most cases, you will face a number of turning points. In general, there are two kinds of turning points. One is the change that occurs inside your mind. You may suddenly lose interest in what you have been doing and take up a new interest. This change of mind is one such opportunity.

Another change occurs when meeting someone new. Some people may not meet anyone new for a whole year, but that would be very rare; the majority meet new people every year as they lead normal, social lives. We definitely meet new people each and every year. People who were complete strangers a year ago suddenly come into our lives, and new relationships form.

These turning points are extremely important. Ultimately, these two types of changes—the changes of the mind and the changes in life that occur as a result of meeting a new person—are opportunities for someone who started from the ordinary to be pushed toward success.

Whether or not you can make courageous decisions when such new developments emerge largely depends on the store of knowledge and experience you have accumulated until that point. If your accumulation is truly worthwhile, you will be able to exert a greater force of energy. However, if your store is lacking, you will most likely miss the opportunity.

One must have plenty of knowledge and experiences, much like how a dam has plentiful water in its reservoir. Only then can the dam generate great power when the water is released. The difference in water levels produces energy, which turns the turbines to generate large amounts of electricity. Here lies a vital key.

In other words, as you make efforts every day and strive to improve yourself, you should also try to grasp new opportunities and find new paths to take. It is important that you cherish the fresh sensations within your mind and the encounters with new people. In many cases, it is usually at such times that your guardian spirit sends you inspiration.

There are times when your sense of values changes completely, either spontaneously in your mind or after meeting someone new.

When you are faced with such a moment, please know that you are currently at a turning point in your destiny. I myself have experienced such moments a number of times. It is important that you try to understand what destiny is trying to teach you every time this happens. It is also an opportunity to take on a new challenge for yourself and check who you are.

6

Courage and Self-Awareness

I have spoken on the importance of new developments. When an opportunity presents itself, it is essential to have courage and self-awareness.

No one has ever achieved great works in life without courage. By courage, I do not mean recklessness or foolhardiness; courage here means the outflowing of energy an ordinary person exerts at a life-changing opportunity.

There are actually many people in the world who intend to assign you to a better position or are willing to guide you to success when the opportunity arises. It would be wonderful if you could meet their expectations. This is when courage is needed. You do not need to fret over how intimidated or weak-willed you are by nature. All you need to do is release the energy you have stored and push yourself forward, just as a dam releases water to turn the turbines.

At such times, self-awareness is important; you need to always remain conscious of what you are doing without being complacent. If you become self-absorbed, you will lose sight of what you are trying to achieve. Even as you act decisively and courageously, you must be aware of your situation; you must understand where you are in the scenario of your life, and whether you are in Act One or Act Two in your own life story or whether you are about to start Act Three. You will not be able to achieve success without such an awareness.

Please know that courage and self-awareness are like twins; both are indispensable in creating a new era and adding a new page to your personal spiritual history. I hope you will understand this.

CHAPTER TWO

The Spirit of Being Independent

1

An Independent Mind

This chapter mainly describes my thoughts on the topic of independence. Once we are born on Earth and live as humans, it is most important to have confidence in our own character and take responsibility for it. This will lead us to nurture an independent mind.

Is it good or bad to have a strong sense of independence? You may not necessarily reach a single conclusion just from a superficial understanding of the word "independence." People who started from the ordinary and aspire to achieve great works in this world must all ponder what it means to have an independent mind.

As the word suggests, independence means to depend solely upon oneself. While this may sound simple, it is difficult to practice in reality. There are two reasons for this difficulty. One is that humans cannot survive in this world alone. No matter how independent a person may be, one cannot live without the help and support of other people. This is a hard fact. It is quite difficult to insist on living with an independent mind when faced with this undeniable truth that our lives are sustained by the cooperation and assistance of many others.

Another difficult issue is achieving individual independence while maintaining harmony with others. Highly independent people are often shunned or disliked by others because their determination to be free and independent often makes them appear too aggressive to those around them, seemingly disturbing the harmony of their surroundings.

But the truth is that other people cannot easily see what you are determined to do, what you want to achieve in the future, or what ideals you have. So, here are two options: Will you strive to gain the approval of others by being a "nice person" throughout your entire life, or are you going to live your life to the fullest and be true to yourself? This is a serious wager you must make.

Consider which way of life will be truly beneficial to you and make you feel fully satisfied at the end of your life. Then, the answer will naturally become clear to you. Living the kind of life you want to live, where you can stand on your own feet and grasp success with your own hands, will obviously bring you a much stronger sense of happiness.

In fact, what is important for humans is how much they were able to paint on the canvas called "life." The size of each person's canvas may differ, but what determines one's victory in life is how much art or beauty one has imbued into it. Some people may be content with producing undistinguished artwork to avoid the risk of receiving a bad critique compared to other people. But could you call that a truthful life?

In every era, there are always people who make critical remarks. There are two kinds of critics: one who offers opinions to try and prevent you from doing something with good intentions or out of kindness, and the more irresponsible one who simply criticizes others for the sake of criticism. I have the impression that many successes in the world were nipped in the bud by the words of such irresponsible people. Humans are so weak that they are easily affected by the words of others. They are not strong enough to shake off negative comments and push forward in the direction they want to go. Herein lies the problem.

Nevertheless, I dare say, just go forward. Stand on your own feet and grasp success with your own hands, for this is also the reason why God, or Buddha, sent humans to Earth.

2

Clarifying One's Responsibility

The essential key to understanding independence lies in the concept of responsibility. At the very least, people who cannot take responsibility for their thoughts, speech, and actions cannot be considered to possess the spirit of independence. The spirit of independence begins with taking responsibility.

Being independent does not mean one should lead a comfortable life and take the easier path by dodging one's way through interpersonal relationships. Such a way of life is avoiding one's responsibilities. True independence means accepting responsibilities rather than abandoning them; it means taking a responsible position decisively and remaining accountable until the end. In this sense, it is of the utmost importance to always clarify one's responsibility.

There are times when a project you are working on with other people may end in failure. When this happens, ask yourself if all the blame should be placed on others. To what extent do you share the blame, or to what degree do you think you bear responsibility? It is essential to analyze these things thoroughly and pragmatically. At the very least, it is not possible for you not to bear any responsibility for things that happen around you or involve you. How far you are willing to develop your sense of responsibility is a prerequisite to being independent.

In fact, the caliber of a person is determined by the degree to which he or she can accept responsibility. A company president is considered to be superior to a rank-and-file employee not because of higher pay or a better position, but because of greater responsibility. A clerk has to take responsibility for actions directly involving his or her job, while a company president is responsible for all employees and all actions taken in the name of the company. The president must even be responsible for work he or she could not directly supervise or get involved in.

This may be a common example, but the same could be said of people who are determined to be successful because they are likely the ones aiming to be leaders. Their goals and pursuits may differ; they may be aspiring to start their own business, live as artists, or devote themselves to a religious mission. But at the very least, those who have no will to clarify their responsibility nor any determination to live up to that responsibility cannot carry out work with an independent mind.

When met with failure, some people are quick to push responsibility onto those around them, blame others for bad advice, or simply blame it on bad luck, claiming that their mistake was an unpredictable event. People with such characters are not truly aiming to be independent. These people will most likely go through a miserable experience after setting up their own businesses and end up proving that they are more suited to be employed by others.

The question is how much responsibility you can handle. This should not be just empty words. How much responsibility can you actually shoulder? It is easy to say to subordinates, "Just keep on doing what you think is best. I'll take responsibility," but how many superiors actually take the blame when things go wrong? This is the benchmark by which one's stature is measured.

If possible, it is best to develop a deep sense of responsibility from a very young age. Even children need to be aware of their responsibilities. When losing a fight, some children might make an excuse and say, "That person was too strong" or "I was outnumbered," instead of admitting their own weaknesses. Children with such tendencies will eventually become failures in life.

It is essential to be true to your heart; do not deceive yourself. Be honest with yourself and admit what you think is a failure to be a failure. By recognizing your failure, you can move on to the next step. But if you do not and only blame the circumstances or the people around you, you will never improve.

Honestly admit to your faults, even if they may be disadvantageous to you. This attitude will lead you to develop a highly independent spirit. If you want to be someone with a lofty character and be a great success, you need to clarify where responsibility lies; you need to be clear about your own responsibility and that of others.

But how to judge others in light of their responsibility is a different matter; you need to consider this question from another angle. Recognizing the responsibility of others should not lead you to immediately criticize them or blame them for their mistakes; these are two different issues. Nevertheless, a leader would be considered foolish if he or she were unable to make an intellectual analysis of where responsibility lies. You cannot become a leader unless you can carefully analyze the reasons for failure, investigate its cause, and identify it. Figuring out how to deal with others while weighing their mistakes against their responsibilities is the next issue.

It is my wish that those aiming to be leaders will have the following attitude. Even when other people are at fault for making a mistake, ask yourself if perhaps you could have helped them in some way, or noticed what was happening and offered them some advice on finding a better direction. No matter how small it may be, if you think there was something you could have done or advice you could have given beforehand, do not blame them for their mistake. Instead, admit your lack of awareness or insight. I believe this kind of attitude is extremely important.

3

Lessons for Self-Improvement

I have talked about the importance of having an independent mind and being able to clarify one's responsibility. What is essential here is to learn the lessons for self-improvement from various occurrences.

Whether it is your own failure or the failure of others, there will always be lessons in the events that happen around you. It is extremely important to learn all you can from these experiences. In fact, those who are able to learn more lessons from the textbook called "life" will eventually become people with great character. Even if people hear the same words, they understand them differently depending on how they interpret them.

There is a saying: "Casting pearls before swine." I do not really like this saying because it is demeaning to pigs, but it should be noted that humans can often be found in similar situations. From the perspective of God or Buddha, humans can be so ignorant as to overlook the "pearls" granted to them; they only accept what they think is beneficial to them and neglect, disapprove of, or try to forget what they think is not.

There is another saying: "Do not cry over spilled milk." This proverb is certainly correct in that getting upset over something that already happened will not fix the situation. But a lesson can certainly be learned from the event. First, it is important to ask yourself why such a failure or mistake has occurred. Thoroughly analyze the process, and be determined not to make the same mistake again. Do not fall into the same pattern of failure. Next, take all the preventive measures to avoid that pattern. This is the way to learn the lessons for self-improvement from various events.

That being said, learning lessons for self-improvement is actually very hard because it is difficult to take a step back and look at yourself objectively. You can realize you have fallen into the same pattern of failure only when you look at yourself from a detached position. Some people always fail when faced with a certain kind of situation because they have formed a set pattern of failure. Every time a similar situation arises, they always end up following the same pattern, even if the situation involves different people, a different place, and a different environment. They fall into the same pattern of failure they experienced in the past and become stuck.

This topic reminds me of a childhood experience. One day, I was playing in a gully near my house. It was easy to climb down, but difficult to climb up. It was only about two meters deep (about 6.5 feet), but it appeared very deep to me at the time since I was still about half as tall as the gully. I went down carefully and reached the bottom, but then I found myself unable to get out. As I was helplessly figuring out what to do, the sun began to set. I called out to a passerby and asked the person to go get my mother. I still remember vividly how my mother, who appeared after a little while, reached down into the gully, grabbed my hand, and pulled me out quite easily.

I felt pity for myself; I was miserable and helpless. I felt lonely to be left all alone. On the other hand, my mother seemed so big, strong, and reliable. I can nostalgically recall the hand of my mother. Her body and soul are much smaller than I am now, but I felt her to be very powerful at the time.

About a year later, I was playing in a completely different place with some other children. We were on a hill, and I accidentally slid down the hill and fell down a steep concrete gutter that ran along the bottom of the hill. I struggled in the dark and tried to scramble out of the sloped gutter, but I did not get very far. I thought of calling out for my mother again, but I was too far away to call for her. The other children were making a fuss above me, but no one tried to help me. I imagined my mother coming and reaching out her hand, but I was determined to somehow get out of the steep gutter myself. I remember using my elbows to nudge myself out little by little.

I felt the texture of the moss and its dampness in the dark. I felt relieved as I gradually managed to raise my head out of the gutter; my arms seemed to move independently as if they were someone else's. It was a great joy to have been able to eventually succeed in climbing out of the cement tunnel on my own, though I initially thought it was beyond my ability. I no longer needed to call for my mother. Once my upper body was out, the rest was not so difficult. The other children were just watching, and on seeing me climbing out, they realized there was no point in laughing at me or making a fuss. After I made my escape, I carried on playing as if nothing had happened. I can recall myself from that day as if it were yesterday.

That was when I came to understand that I should not expect help from someone else every time even if I was once saved before. I should do as much as possible within my own ability. There may be times when I am not able to solve the problem by myself and have no choice but to ask for help from others, but first I must do as much as I can on my own. I learned how important it is to have such an attitude. This was when I was about eight. I believe it also served as a lesson to improve myself.

4

Financial Awareness

When considering independence, I cannot avoid touching on financial matters since financial awareness is important for human beings.

About 2,600 years ago, Shakyamuni Buddha walked around India teaching people the Truth. But just after leaving the royal palace in Kapilavastu, he started living like a beggar; the luxurious life he once had as a prince was of no more use to him. He then chose to live by receiving food and alms from others. He set aside a part of each day to receive alms while spending the rest of his day in meditation, teaching people the Truth, and contemplating ways to enrich the mind. This was the starting point of Buddhism. However, about 2,600 years have passed since then. What kind of financial awareness do we need now in order to live a truthful life in contemporary society?

I am convinced that financial independence is also essential for human beings. There may be many people who consider money as evil and impure, and feel ashamed to even think about it, but I think such a way of thinking is too extreme and narrow-minded. When coins were made of gold in the past, money had real value on its own, but today money is printed on paper which has little intrinsic value. This means that the significance of money lies elsewhere; money is important because it is one way to measure value.

How can value in this world be measured? It is based on the general rule of appropriately rewarding any useful material or services provided. Whether we provide material or services to a person, animal, or plant, we receive an equivalent reward in return.

So, the essential point here is for you to have a certain degree of confidence in your financial situation. One may certainly feel free of attachment when living off charity from other people, but such way of life would be ignoring the economic principles that are necessary in establishing oneself in society. By this, I do not mean earning easy money, but it is important to truly contribute to society and do helpful work, receiving appropriate acknowledgment, and accumulating a reputation for good work.

I have often seen how lack of money can affect and deteriorate people's minds. Unfortunately, people cannot use money if they do not have it, but if they have it, in many cases they tend to use it to control others. So, if you want to establish a spirit of independence and live your life based on this spirit, it is important that you are economically independent as well.

Being financially independent means there will at least be no risk of being forced to change your convictions by the power of money; it means your religious beliefs or passion for the Truth will not be affected by other people's money. Based on this idea, I have created a new Buddha Sangha (group of disciples) because people who work in religion and live for the Truth can never be spiritually independent in the truest sense if they are enslaved by the wealth of others.

Someone once said that one should not make a living through religious activities. Although this claim represents partial truth, there is currently no system in Japan that provides financial support to those devoting themselves to the exploration of the Truth. If such a system existed, they could use it to support themselves, but since it does not currently exist, it is very important that we protect our fortresses of Truth on our own. For this reason, I place importance on having an economically stable foundation when teaching the Truth in modern times. I also encourage everyone to do so.

You must not be bound by the feeling of guilt over money or let your mind waver. To build an unshakable mind, you need to have confidence. In other words, it is important that you have unwavering confidence in the fact that you are contributing to society through your thoughts and your work. It is my wish that people who live for the Truth are economically independent, financially well-off, and affluent enough so they will not be deluded by money. I also hope they will gain higher public recognition as they achieve higher enlightenment and become of greater service to more people.

From ancient times, money has been regarded as something evil, and even today it comes with the risk of temptation. At the same time, it is also true that money can motivate people to improve themselves.

Starting from the ordinary can also mean beginning from poverty. It is a question of how a person who began with no money or property becomes someone of importance and starts to have a positive influence on a large number of people in the world. I hope people with enlightenment, or people who have studied the Truth, will gain stronger financial power and use it to exert a positive influence on people around the world. I believe this to be a wonderful thing.

Achieving a financial state that is neither in the red nor in the black is not enough. Try to gain greater financial power, and use your resources and your wealth as tools to lead the people of the world in the right direction. Such a way of life is possible. I want to promote this way of thinking in modern society. Economic power can be used as a weapon to protect yourself and to improve the world. Unless we boost our financial power and use it in this direction, feelings of guilt concerning money will only increase. It is my sincere wish that you will value this kind of financial awareness and understanding of Truth-based economics.

5

Keeping Promises

I have just covered the topic of financial awareness, and the next important attitude is keeping promises. There can be any number of factors that may prevent you from acting on your initial intentions, but what is essential is the fact that you have tried to do everything you could to keep your commitments. There may be times when you find it difficult to keep a promise you made verbally, but what matters is that you spoke with an honest heart.

Keeping a promise can sometimes mean abiding by the law. About 2,400 years ago, before Socrates took a cup of poisonous hemlock, he commented, "A law is a law however undesirable it may be." Socrates believed that as long as he was an Athenian citizen, he was bound by Athenian law. Even though it might have been a bad law, he considered evading it to be the same as breaking it and therefore a denial of his obligation as a good citizen.

Leaving aside the question of whether or not Socrates showed the right attitude, it is at least true that civilizations exist on the condition that people abide by certain rules. As long as people are expected to follow the rules, it is wrong to break them in principle.

However, there is something I want you to consider here, and that is, "The most important promise for humans is the one they make to God." Promises made between humans are shallow and have little significance. On the other hand, the promise between humans and God is extremely profound and has deep significance.

The fact that humans have been blessed with life on Earth means we bear responsibility in the face of God. The very fact that we have been given life by God comes with responsibility.

So, what exactly is the responsibility we have taken on? It is our promise to live our lives as the children of God and with the Will of God as our own. Such a promise has been made. It is not possible for us to be reborn on Earth without having made this promise to God. Although there are differences in degree, we all have made a promise before being reborn on Earth that we would be of service to God and abide by His teachings.

It is wrong to do evil because it means one would be breaking the promise made to God. Humans are humans because they have made a promise to God to be so. That is why souls are allowed to live in human form. If we break our promise to God, we never know when we will cease to live as humans.

Please know that we were born as humans and are now living as humans because of our promise to God. I hope many people will learn about this truth. To those of you who ask why it is necessary to practice love, mercy, and justice as God commands, it is because you have made a promise. That is the prerequisite of being human.

Human souls will suffer when they break this promise. This suffering is called hell, and it is where many souls suffer in agony. They suffer from the feeling of remorse for having broken the promise or the vows they made because they themselves and their consciences are unable to forgive what they have thought and done. That is why they try hard to make amends for their past wrongdoings in hell.

I repeat: The greatest promise humans have made is the one made to God. This promise takes effect when one is born on Earth. It is the promise to abide by the words of God and to live accordingly. Everyone has made this promise.

Independence does not mean independence from God. It means to fulfill the promise you have made to God as your responsibility. This is what is meant by independence. The true meaning of the spirit of independence is to fulfill your promise to God as you live your life based on your individual character.

Here are the questions I want each of you to ask your heart: "What kind of promise did I make to God? How did I make this vow?" When you think about this, please also consider what it means for you to keep that promise and to carry it out. Then you will realize that this was a promise to use your strengths to the fullest to benefit the people of the world, while simultaneously preventing your weaknesses from affecting others negatively or hindering others' work. The promise one has made to God differs depending on each individual. But it is extremely important to always remember the fact that you have made a promise to God.

6

Standing Alone and Walking on Your Own

I have discussed the spirit of independence from various angles. Lastly, I would like to discuss the idea of standing alone and walking on your own.

Imagine the wish parents have for their children. They most probably pray for their children to ultimately live independent, happy lives. While humans have made promises to God to live their lives on Earth, God ultimately wishes for everyone to live brilliant, colorful lives in a world of self-reliance and with the Will of God as their own. This is the true meaning of standing alone and walking on your own.

Live out your own unique life, while treasuring your promise to God. In the course of living your distinctive life, do not break your promise to God. On this point, be clear about your responsibility. If you break your promise, reflect on what you did wrong, learn new lessons from the mistake, and develop greater strength to continue moving forward. This is the way of life that is expected of humans. I hope you will value the spirit of standing alone and walking on your own, which is the spirit of courageously making the most of your character.

In doing so, remember that in the eyes of God, you appear like one of the particles of God's Light of seven colors. You may also appear like a beautiful flower-shaped firework that blooms in the summer night sky. When fireworks explode, beautiful petals of light spread across the night sky. Each of these petals represents you living in the spirit of independence. Although each petal scatters independently, the petals together create a greater, harmonious pattern. Because the flower-shaped firework is not made of a single light but of many colorful lights scattered across the sky, it appears to create greater harmony.

In the same way, the fact that everyone has his or her own unique character and lives a life of self-reliance does not mean people are traveling a self-centered road. Seen from a grander, artistic point of view, everyone is contributing to creating greater harmony in the world. In the process of taking the path to creating greater harmony, you live in self-reliance—standing alone and walking on your own—while exerting yourself to your utmost as a child of God. Please know this fact.

It is my hope for you to take a fresh look at yourself from the perspective of God and live your own life with courage. I pray that more and more people will live in this way.

CHAPTER THREE

Diverse Values

1

Understanding People

This chapter is on the topic of diverse values, which is closely related to my fundamental way of thinking. Whether or not a person is capable of accepting diverse values is associated with the person's philosophy. In general, philosophers tend to put forth a simple, powerful idea and deny all other ideas, but I have a somewhat different attitude. While I intend to adhere to my ideas as my own, if there are things to be gained from other ideas, I am willing to learn and absorb them.

After all, this attitude is connected to how one looks at people and the world. In other words, people who believe their own ideas and ways of thinking to be the only truths and deny everything else tend to judge others based on the thought, "Those people I find to be beneficial or pleasant to me are good, but all others are not." However, as long as they look at people in this way, they cannot say they have truly understood others. Understanding others means you are looking at them with boundless love, and looking at others with love means you cannot help but take an interest in them. That is how things are.

Can you claim to have understood a person completely? I am sure you cannot. Understanding a person is difficult, indeed. Each individual possesses qualities that endlessly pique other people's interests and boundless potential hidden within. The amount of information and experiences stored within a person equals the amount found in a library, or even surpasses it. Just as we cannot read all the books in a library, it is impossible to know all of the thoughts and experiences of an individual. Therefore, what matters when looking at others is how much you can take an interest in them and learn from them.

There is a huge difference between those who observe others with the intent of learning something from them, and those who simply look at others without much thought. Some people do not try to learn from others at all, or do so only when they find it beneficial to themselves, but otherwise pay them no attention. These people will eventually realize how wasteful and foolish it was to have thrown away something of so much value.

Sources of learning are not limited to school textbooks. Everything, including the things you find in your surroundings and the people you encounter in the course of your life, can be great sources to learn from. How you make good use of them and apply them to your own life will determine whether your life will ultimately end in success or failure.

2

Taking an Interest

From a relatively early age, I have had a deep interest in people. The reason I took great interest in others was probably because I was deeply curious about myself as well; I was interested in my inner self. As I grew older, my personality became more introverted and I started thinking more deeply about things. My tendency to ponder over my own worries inevitably turned into observing other people.

"What are the differences between my character and the characters of others? What caused these differences? Why have these differences manifested in such a way? How did we come to have different ways of thinking?" I began to think about these kinds of questions.

When I was young, I believed my thoughts were independent and resulted from my own unique character traits, but I eventually came to realize that my ways of thinking were strongly influenced by my parents. As a teenager, however, I could not fully perceive how much influence my parents had on me and how much of my perspective was limited and controlled by their ways of thinking.

I began to understand this after I turned 20. When I started to reflect on what I said and thought from the perspective of a third party, I came to realize that many of my words and thoughts were similar to those of my father and mother, and I was astounded.

When I interacted with people based on the assumption that the sense of values I had held since childhood was normal, I found that others reacted differently. Upon seeing their reactions, I noticed that even the thoughts I found to be normal and right were not necessarily true for them. This led me to start questioning things, even though I did not necessarily think like René Descartes. I thought the values I had were normal, but other people did not necessarily believe the same. So, I began to wonder if the values I held were actually normal or whether they were wrong. As I thought more deeply on this matter, I gradually realized that there was a great difference between my ideas, beliefs, and ways of thinking and those of other people.

Let me give you an example. I was brought up in a religious environment from my early years. Both of my parents believed in Buddha and God, and I thought it was normal to believe in the existence of spirits. I think I was in my fifth year of primary school when I first experienced a clash of values with another person on this matter.

The female homeroom teacher in the classroom next to mine could be described as a "go-getter"; she was apparently active in the Japan Teachers' Union. One day, she stopped me and asked, "You say you believe in a world after death and that spirits exist, but on what grounds are you saying those things?" This teacher questioned me from her perspective of not believing in things that cannot be proven.

I thought it was indeed difficult to prove. But there were many people who had seen spirits or experienced some spiritual phenomena, and I knew a fair number of people in my surroundings who had also had actual spiritual experiences, so I tried to support my belief by sharing such examples. However, the teacher replied that she could not believe in things she could not experience for herself. At the time,

I felt keenly the difficulty of proving spiritual matters or convincing others of them.

My classmates, who were still at an innocent age, would listen to me speak about my beliefs without raising any particular objections, regardless of whether or not they believed what I said. Maybe it was because there were still many people who sympathized with spiritual beliefs in a place like our town, which was surrounded by mountains, on Shikoku Island. Many of my classmates claimed to have seen will-o'-the-wisps on their way home from school, while others had seen ghosts. Given those circumstances and the rural environment, I did not stand out much.

Later, however, when I began my studies at the University of Tokyo after high school, I found that people around me held completely different values. There were simply very few people who candidly believed in the world of spirits like I did. Many people even seemed to think that such a belief was a rebellion against the intelligentsia, or almost like treason against the intellect.

One of my close friends was a Christian. He was a Catholic, but to my surprise, he did not really believe in spirits. I could hardly believe this and was deeply shocked. Although he said he was a pious Catholic, he had a different idea about spirits. As I observed his behavior, I felt that his faith in religion was more like an adherence to a moral code. While he would strongly follow his religion's precepts and discipline, the subject of spirits was of no interest to him. Moreover, he seemed to believe that God could only be sensed in Jesus' time, but not in today's world. I had a very strange feeling when I heard that. I was surprised that there were people with religious faith who did not know anything about spirits or could not perceive the presence of spirits.

I had another friend who said he could never believe in the existence of spirits. When we had discussions about spirits, he said, "If spirits exist, how are they created when babies are born? How can a spirit be formed through birth? Their primary source of existence cannot be explained." So, I told him that spirits exist prior to birth, undergo reincarnation, and are reborn numerous times, but he could not believe my explanation. He retorted, "If you say spirits living in the other world have high intellect, then why do they enter an infant's body and just cry? That's hard to believe." He believed humans evolved from apes, which had evolved from amoebae. Unfortunately, this seems to be the mainstream idea of present times.

It was a great shock to me. From childhood, I had learned about faith and religious sense as a matter of course from my parents' beliefs, so I sensed a huge gap. Upon consideration, however, maybe it cannot be helped that people come to have such ideas because they do not officially learn about spiritual matters in the Japanese education system.

Since then, I have maintained the interests I took at the time. I discovered that my personal ways of thinking, believing, or understanding things may not always be shared by everyone. I also learned that convincing others of religious truths requires a very difficult process. There is actually a great difference between those who are able to instinctively believe in spiritual matters and those who cannot.

My ongoing challenge is to figure out how to prove spiritual matters. However, at the very least, I can say that there will not be any further philosophical development for those who cannot calmly observe others' feelings or understand how others perceive them or their ways of thinking.

3

Discovering Wonderful Aspects

I thus learned that other people's thinking was greatly different from mine. But even if others had different ideas concerning an issue or belief, I did not disregard them or think there was nothing I could learn from them. I have met quite a few atheists, but there were things to be learned from them as well. I learned a number of things from materialists, too. As a result of these experiences, I realized we should not put labels on people.

People are apt to put labels on others. I would often notice this even after I started working. When I was a first-year employee, there was a man who explained the workplace to me. When he described his colleagues, he would point out what kind of person each of them was based on his own labels. However, due to my natural interest in others, I wanted to know more about the people who were shunned or bullied by others, so I started to join these people for lunch or for coffee.

Then, interestingly, the other colleagues started perceiving me to be a close friend or a member of the group they did not like, and therefore different from them. That was my second surprise. I learned that many people think, "Friends of people we dislike are not likely to be our friends, but the friends of those we like would be our friends." On the other hand, I felt that liking or not liking a particular person should be up to each individual, and that one's sense of values could not necessarily be shared with others.

According to what I learned from political science, the German jurist Carl Schmitt had similar views on enemies and supported the idea that "the enemy of my enemy is my friend." Such dichotomous thinking was commonly observed in real society. This felt strange to me, but I realized that sometimes people failed to judge or evaluate others based on their own independent sense of value.

Personally, if I like person A, I do not expect person B to also like person A. I think it is up to person B to like person A or not. In the same way, even if I do not like person A, I do not expect everyone else to also dislike person A. Person B may like person A, whereas person C may dislike person A. I have taken this kind of stance, but I realized that this way of thinking is very peculiar in Japanese society because Japanese people tend to form a conformist mindset and ostracize anyone who appears different.

I have learned many lessons from such experiences. I think I especially learned a lot from the comments of those who were disliked or belittled by others. In reality, there are many aspects to a person that are different from what can be understood by the simple perception of whether one is a friend or foe, or part of the group or not. You cannot accept the label people have placed on others as the definite truth.

As I wrote in Chapter Two, I was earnestly seeking to obtain the spirit of independence, so I maintained the attitude that I would learn what should be learned and discard what should be discarded, based on my own beliefs. However, other people seemed unable to understand this attitude.

After all, being willing to know someone or something ultimately leads you to take an interest in that person or thing, and your interest will eventually lead you to make wonderful discoveries. You will be able to see how wonderful a person is or discover something you have never known before; you will gain such an acute sense of understanding, and you will be moved by it.

Why do you have to hold the same set of values as others? Why do you have to label someone in the same way others have? Why not try to remove such labels?

At times, my actions and way of thinking certainly put me in disadvantageous positions and caused misunderstandings. Misunderstandings inevitably arose because some people did not comprehend the diverse values I had when interacting with others. Even so, I still retain this approach to this day. As the CEO of Happy Science, I am surrounded by many people, but there is no one I dislike. I see their good points and appreciate them.

However, some people have a different sense of value. For example, when I praise someone, they may think, "I'm the only one who is special to Master. I'm sure Master doesn't like the others as much as me," or "I am different from the others. Master likes me, which should mean he does not like the others. Master treats me and only me favorably." There are people who tend to think like this. When I found this to be true soon after establishing Happy Science, I was really shocked.

I am capable of treating each person favorably based on who they are. But there are people who are incapable of doing this in reality. There are those who are quick to assume being favored means that they are the only ones being liked, and no one else. I believe this is a common way of thinking.

Basically, I have adopted an attitude of trying to discover the wonderful aspects of each person. As a result, I have been able to discover and sense the wonderful aspects of each Law whenever I teach the Truth. As I acknowledge and accept the differences in the teachings, I have been discovering the shining qualities within each one. I have also learned that even if some ideas do not apply to me personally, they can be beneficial to other people. I have thus experienced such a philosophical development.

My attitudes of taking a personal interest and discovering new sets of values eventually contributed to developing my own philosophy. At the very least, this attitude has provided me with a form of wealth. I still believe this has enriched my way of thinking.

4

Thinking about Good and Evil

I have talked about taking an interest in diverse values and discovering wonderful aspects, which now leads us to the next topic: how to think about good and evil. This is the most important issue a religious leader must face. It is the question of how to approach the ideas of good and evil. The ideas of good and evil are extremely difficult; for religious leaders, it may be as challenging as being asked what enlightenment is. A person's entire philosophical outlook can be revealed in answering the question "What are good and evil?"

I have learned that an individual's sense of values can be quite different even in the world of high spirits. Even the spirits that are regarded as bodhisattvas or tathagatas can sometimes have different ways of thinking. That was another discovery for me. I think this kind of discovery has not been found in conventional religions.

Normally, each religious leader adheres to a single god, such as a divine god he or she believes in, a guiding spirit, or Buddha, and regards that god's particular teachings as absolute truth. They then consider other ideas that do not accord with their teachings to be heresy. However, I have shown through books published by Happy Science that high spirits sometimes have different opinions. This means that good and evil can no longer be distinguished on a two-dimensional plane as is conventionally considered; instead, the ideas of good and evil have expanded into a three-dimensional space. In other words, it has become clear that there are height, width, and depth to the ideas of good and evil.

The height indicates the level of good and evil; there is certainly a heavenly realm and a hellish realm in the spiritual world, or the Real World. This is the traditional idea of good and evil. But I have also learned that good and evil exist on a horizontal plane as well. Different values can exist even within the heavenly world.

For example, many Christians believe that their religion is the only truth and that Jesus Christ is the only Son of God or God's envoy. When these people encounter Buddhists or followers of other religions, there is room for the devotees of the two religions to view each other as evil. This is because they do not know or understand each other. This lack of knowledge and understanding leads one to consider the other as evil.

Therefore, while the ideas of good and evil basically mean good vibrations and evil vibrations, just as heaven and hell are separated under the Laws of Buddha, or the Laws of the Universe, they can also be conflicting vibrations due to the lack of understanding. I gradually came to understand that evil can arise from people's inability to understand or agree with one another.

From this, we can see that good and evil must be considered on a spatial plane. In fact, we cannot tell whether someone is good or evil, or whether someone's words or actions are good or evil, unless we identify that person's level of enlightenment. In the case of someone who has yet to awaken to the Truth, it is extremely difficult to judge whether his or her way of thinking is good or bad. It is very difficult indeed. You cannot say someone is evil simply because that person does not have the same level of awareness as you do.

As you raise your level of awareness, you will be able to see more aspects of other people. When you notice the good and bad parts of other people, can you put yourself in their position and sympathize with their ideas? Or will you just judge them as evil for not being on the same level of enlightenment as you? There is such a difference in perspective.

If you look at how mothers and older women talk to children, you will see something peculiar about how they speak. Their speech is completely different from how they usually converse with other adults. They use simple terms and adapt their speech to the children. In this way, they are adjusting themselves to the people they are talking to. In fact, there may be a key to transcending the matter of good and evil here. The primary cause for good and evil to arise is one's inability to adjust oneself to others or sympathize with others. So, it is important to consider how to put yourself in the other person's position and understand them.

5

A Consideration of Dichotomy

I have spoken about good and evil, and now we need to give a second thought to the idea of dichotomy. People like to think about things in black and white. There are also people who think about things based on a trichotomy; they think in black, white, and gray. But I, myself, do not base my thinking on either a dichotomy or a trichotomy.

The reason that good and evil arise may perhaps come from people's tendency to think of things based on dichotomies, such as "yes or no" or "left or right." In the world of "yes or no," good and evil will certainly emerge. And if we shift away from the world of "yes or no" to accept a more pluralistic world or one with diverse values, we are faced with the subsequent issue of how to integrate these values. Integrating different values is the difficult part.

It is easy to organize our thoughts based on a dichotomy, but reconciling diverse ways of thinking is quite challenging. In this sense, dichotomous thinking is certainly simple in terms of efficacy. However, I think there is a fundamental problem in this way of thinking. While it is the simplest way of judging others, it also omits many important aspects. For example, if a fruit has some bruises, the question arises of whether to remove the bad part and eat the rest or to throw out the entire fruit. By thinking based on a dichotomy, you will consider a bruised banana or persimmon to be "rotten" and throw the whole fruit away.

To solve this problem, I usually consider things based on the coordinate axis of "time." Even if things are currently classified as black or white, or good or evil, they can change over a certain period of time. I leave room for such possibility.

I do not think there are people who are good throughout their lives, or people who are evil from birth to death. Isn't it the true nature of humans to do good at times and do wrong at other times? So, the key to overcoming dichotomous thinking is found along the axis of time, or in the flow of time, not at one point in time. This is exactly how God or Buddha sees people and the world.

From ancient times, people have questioned why evil exists on Earth, why hell exists in the other world, and why Satan exists if God exists as the only absolute, perfect Being. This has been a big issue, but no one has ever been able to give a clear answer. To answer these questions, the perspective of time needs to be considered. What may appear to be evil in one slice of time can change into something different over a longer period of time.

Take, for example, the Meiji Restoration that took place in Japan over a century ago. Battles between those loyal to the emperor and those loyal to the shogunate were fought all over Japan. At that time, what was the determining factor of good and evil? Were those fighting for the emperor good and those fighting for the shogunate evil? Let us consider this case.

Just like the proverb "Might is right," the imperial forces, who were the ultimate victors, were considered at the time to have justice on their side. However, 50 or even 100 years prior to that era, it was considered right to fight for the shogunate and wrong to rebel or plot against it. Despite that, at the time of the Meiji Restoration, the alliance between the Satsuma, Choshu, Tosa, and Hizen clans, which fought against the shogunate, was ultimately evaluated positively as being just. So, how should this evaluation be viewed?

Did people who sided with the shogunate until the end consider themselves evil? At the time, the opposing alliance upheld the emperor's virtue as a banner of righteousness and used it as a symbol. In this way, people were concerned from ancient times about who God or Buddha would side with. At turning points in history, it is often difficult to tell where justice lay without perceiving which side God or Buddha would support.

However, whether the Meiji Restoration was good or evil was also decided over the course of time; if the newly formed Meiji government had turned out to be a terrible administration, the forces of the shogunate may have regained power and the new government could have been overthrown. If that had happened, the fighting of the imperial forces would have probably been regarded as a traitorous rebellion. From this we can say that the decisive factor that distinguishes good and evil is found with the passage of time. We can also say that a conflict of values occurring at a certain point in time is actually a movement to create a new era.

It is like the waves that wash up onto a beach. Waves come in from the open sea and break on the shore, but not all waves necessarily come straight to shore. As the first waves recede from the beach, they push back against the next waves, so the newly formed waves cannot reach the shore unless they pass over the previous ones. In this way, the earlier waves flow back against the new waves, so the new waves must overcome the earlier ones to accomplish their goal of reaching the shore.

Perhaps the clashes in values throughout history, or the conflicts between different philosophies and activities during the transition to a new era, are like waves on the shore. If the receding waves are stronger, the new waves will not be able to reach the beach. This is how I see things.

6

Thoughts on Monism

Another interesting way of thinking is monism, or the monism of Light. It is said to be a part of Japanese Shinto philosophy. Masaharu Taniguchi* also taught that everything can be reduced to the monism of Light. His basic idea was, "There is no such thing as conflict between the dichotomous values of good and evil; there is essentially only light in the world. Darkness does not exist, for it will disappear when light is held high."

Basically, this idea is the same as the New Thought philosophy that arose in the United States. Such beliefs of enlightenment and positive thinking follow the same line of thought. The famous philosopher Ralph Waldo Emerson also adopted this way of thinking. He supported the idea that "There is no such thing as hot or cold; cold is just an absence of heat. If something is deprived of heat, it will automatically become cold. So, cold is not an absolute value." This is a monistic way of thinking.

However, I think it is difficult to understand this way of thinking as an actual, substantial theory because there is an illogical side to this philosophy. While it is true that darkness disappears with light, can you truly say that night is merely the absence of daytime? Some people may believe that night is merely the absence of the sun

---

* TF: Masaharu Taniguchi (1893–1985) was the founder of the Japanese religious organization Seicho-no-Ie.

and that, therefore, night essentially does not exist. However, day and night existed 1,000, 10,000, and even 100 million years ago, so is it really possible to conclude that something that has always existed throughout history is not real?

Here I find some distortion in the philosophy; it is a way of thinking based merely on the wording. I think it is more rational to accept what actually exists as real and consider ways to interpret it.

No matter how earnestly you may insist that night does not exist, your argument would be futile. If you claim, "There is no such thing as the cold. It is merely the absence of heat," when it is snowing or the water is freezing outside, people will only think you are pretending to endure the cold out of pride. Those living in colder regions will perhaps find your words ridiculous.

It is very difficult for people to think about things from a perspective that is separate from their current standpoint. Even if they are told about the Real World or the True World, they can hardly understand what is being said because they know nothing about it.

Furthermore, even the realms of tathagatas and bodhisattvas in the Real World are not monistic in reality. While these are the realms of Light, there is an undeniable fact that Light is not monistic; there is not just one kind of Light. The truth is that Light manifests itself in different ways. Once we know this, we will come to understand that the thought of monism contains very difficult ideas.

After all, monism essentially means that there is only a single source of Light. Even if there is only one source, Light can be transmitted in many different ways. When there is an obstruction, a shadow is projected. When light is blocked by a paper screen, it cannot pass unless there is a hole in the screen. In this way, even if there is only a single Light source, how Light travels or manifests itself can be different.

In this context, the monism of Light should be renamed "the monism of the source of Light." This is the idea that the Light source is monistic; there is only one source of Light, and everything originates from one source. With regard to this, there is no mistake. However, if it is taken to mean that there can be nothing but Light around us because there is only one Light source, then that is too extreme. Nevertheless, there is something about the idea of the monism of Light or the monism of goodness that cannot be dismissed altogether when considering its effectiveness.

There is another idea that says, "Evil can amplify, enlarge, and manifest itself in reality when it is recognized, so it is best not to admit it." This way of thinking actually contains one aspect of Truth. There are cases where evil can flare up by gaining recognition, as if adding fuel to a fire.

However, there is also a problem with this idea: the issue of retributive punishment as described in criminal law. Criminal law is based on the idea that one must atone for the crimes one has committed, so how should this idea be understood? This issue will lead us to consider the idea of legalism (the rule of law) that arose in the process of modernization.

If we look at societal laws, it is obvious that they are not based on the monism of Light or the monism of goodness. It is very clear that laws have been created from the standpoint of dualism. This is not only true of criminal law but also of civil law, commercial law, and labor law. With the assumption that conflicts will occur, these laws describe the various methods for settling them. All laws are created on the premise that conflicts might occur and evil can arise. So, how should we understand these laws?

To begin with, if the Laws of Buddha or God were meant to solely praise people or just to say that all people are good, there would not be a need for precepts or commandments. The promises between humans and Buddha or God would not exist. But because there is a promise, the potential act of breaking the promise exists. If there were no promise from the outset, then there would be no act of breaking it. This is an extremely difficult issue.

While there is an idea that evil can be amplified by gaining recognition, it is also possible that evil can increase when it is not recognized as evil. For example, if burglars were regarded as good-natured in essence, and were treated kindly for such qualities, then they would continue to commit one evil after another. Therefore, although it is true that there is only one source of Light or Law, it can manifest itself in various ways downstream. That is why we need to convince others according to each person's level of awareness.

I think the monism of goodness or the monism of Light holds true to a large extent for people who have a fairly high level of awareness. It should be a convincing idea for such people. However, those who have not yet reached that level of awareness need to be taught what good and evil are. It is essential to teach them what it is that they must not do. This is one of the purposes of education.

So, I think the most rational way of thinking is as follows: In the first stage, when one's soul is still very young and its level of awareness and enlightenment is still low, it is best to learn what is good and what is bad, what accords with the Will of God or Buddha and what does not. Once one has attained a full understanding of the dichotomy of good and evil, it is best to move on to adopt the monistic way of thinking and try to understand that what seems to be good or evil is seen differently in the eyes of God or Buddha. As you shift from the dualistic view to the monistic view in this way, you need to take "the passage of time" into consideration. This attitude is very important.

Start with the dualistic view, and then adopt the concept of "the passage of time" to see things from the standpoint of "relative dualism." Eventually, move on to embrace the monistic view. This process is the true way of understanding the Truth and good and evil.

7

The Radiance of Truth

I have discussed a variety of subjects, and I would now like to talk about "the radiance of Truth," which we often experience while observing people or studying the teachings. These experiences will bring us endless joy.

I have encountered many Truths and talked with many high spirits, and it has been my greatest joy to have experienced the radiance of various Truths on every occasion. Even ideas that are not philosophically high-level can emit a light of Truth. The more you bathe in such radiance of Truth, the higher your enlightenment will become. There are many kinds of joys in life, but I think being able to feel the radiance of various Truths is one form of happiness.

People tend to have a limited way of seeing things. Their outlooks are based on their own fixed ideas, and they think their perception is the only way of viewing things. They often feel a sense of security in seeing things in such a way. However, it would be a great discovery and a huge surprise for them to know that there are other completely different ways of thinking that also contain the Truth. Without experiencing such a surprise, the gates of Truth will not open.

Learning the Truth comes with surprise; without experiencing this surprise, you cannot know the Truth. When you are given opportunities to learn new things—new ways of thinking, new phenomena, or new stimuli—your soul will be greatly astonished, and the skin or shell that was covering your soul will start to shed.

Therefore, you must first sail out into the vast ocean of Truth. On the ocean of Truth, perceive the radiance of Truth. Feel it on your own skin. This is most important.

When you are surprised by various things, or when you are astonished by encounters with the unknown, how can you absorb and incorporate these new values as your own? This is the great challenge left for you to take on. You need to go beyond the level of simply recognizing them as diverse values, and somehow harmonize, integrate, and elevate them into one sublime idea. These efforts are extremely important.

You may end up returning to your starting point as a result of these efforts, but these efforts are by no means futile. Even if you were to return to where you originally set out, there is a tremendous difference between coming back from a journey of the soul with discoveries of the Truth, and coming back without having gained any experiences at all. This difference is the value of experience.

Therefore, I would like you to adopt the following attitudes. One is to enjoy the Laws. To rejoice in perceiving the radiance of various Truths means to enjoy the Laws. I hope you will experience this state of "enjoying the Laws" at least once. The other attitude is to climb the steps of the Laws. Do not neglect this subsequent path. Please know that this road will ultimately take you to God or Buddha.

8

What Lies at the Heart of Diversity

To close this chapter, I would like to touch on what lies at the heart of diversity. What appears as diversity is the result of the limitations of human recognition. The limited vision of the human eye in this three-dimensional world is the perfect example. Human eyes are incapable of fully capturing a three-dimensional object as is. Have you ever thought about this?

The world perceived by human eyes is the same as what appears in a photograph; it is a two-dimensional, planar view. Although we can sense depth, the world we see is exactly the same as one presented in a picture. We can only see it in two dimensions. Therefore, when we look at an object, we cannot see it from all angles simultaneously. That is the way humans are.

Even if we look at a potted plant, for example, we cannot see it from all angles at the same time. We can only see it like a series of camera shots taken from different angles and combine them to recognize an overall image. In the same way, the fact that diversity exists for the Truth is not because the Truth is diverse. Just as there is only one potted plant in the analogy, there is only one Truth; the angles from which we look at it differ.

To use another analogy, there is only one Mt. Fuji. Yet many photographers take pictures of it from different positions, and no two photos are the same. They are all different. Then, can we simply dismiss it as being the result of different perspectives? Can we just conclude that Mt. Fuji can appear in a variety of ways? Even so, Mt. Fuji is Mt. Fuji; it is unique. We need to understand this.

The existence of diverse values does not mean there are many Mt. Fujis. If we forget this point, we will make a serious mistake. There is only one Mt. Fuji, but it is possible for there to be many different pictures of Mt. Fuji when it is photographed. That's all it is.

Therefore, the fact that the Truth can appear in various forms means that there are limitations to human recognition. There is only one Truth, in the same way that there is only one Mt. Fuji. There is only one Reality. There is only one Buddha or God. There is only one teaching of Buddha or God. But because this is multi-dimensional, humans cannot fully understand it with their two-dimensional recognition.

Please remember that it is one great misconception to think, "There is truth in the teaching of relying only on divine salvation and the teaching of relying only on self-power. Buddhism is true, Christianity is true, and Japanese Shinto is true. There are many truths in each of these things."

In fact, there is essentially only one Truth. But due to the limited scope of human recognition, the one Truth can be seen in different forms, depending on "how the photo is taken" or the position or angle from which it is viewed. From the perspective of those with a higher level of awareness or those who can immediately take in the entire picture of righteousness or Truth, there is essentially no such thing as diversity.

"Diversity of recognition" and "diversity of existence" are two different things. Even if there is diversity in recognition, there can only be one existence. Please know this. Diverse values must ultimately lead you to embrace this single value system. I hope you will not make a mistake on this point.

CHAPTER FOUR

Buddha and God—
The Unknown

1

A Longing for Buddha and God

In this chapter, I would like to discuss how I encountered Buddha and God, how I came to think about the Divine, and my belief in spiritual matters before arriving at faith. Before talking about how I came to perceive the presence of Buddha and God, I must touch on my family environment.

One's family environment during childhood is extremely important in developing a religious disposition because young children naturally grow up by listening to what their parents say without harboring any doubt. I also think my parents' belief in Buddha and God was a major factor that led me to have religious faith and to think it was a matter of course to believe in Buddha and God.

I would come to realize the huge difference between my childhood family environment and the external social environment later in my life, but be that as it may, I now feel very lucky to have been able to accept unquestioningly the existence of Buddha and God at a relatively young age. If one spends 20 or 30 years soaking in materialism, it is not easy to suddenly turn one's thoughts to Buddha and God; one would need to undergo some shocking experience to do so. In this sense, perhaps I was quite fortunate.

A family environment may entail a variety of things: a good financial situation, a convenient environment in an urban area, or a large house. But no matter the living environment one grows up in, the most important factor in one's childhood is the kind of influences one received in shaping one's character and views of life. No matter what kind of family environment I was born and raised in, as long as I received appropriate influence to develop my spirituality, I believe I would have eventually started walking down the same road that I am walking now.

As Saint Augustine writes in *Confessions*, even he, a great soul, suffered immensely from the battle between his spirit and body in order to discover the true God. In my case, I was able to accept the ideas of "spirit," "soul," "Buddha," and "God" from an early age without feeling uneasy, so in this respect I was very lucky.

From this we can see that it is vital for the family to plant the seeds of spiritual views of life and faith in Buddha or God in a child's mind. Even as a new religion and its teachings spread around the world, I feel from my own experience that it is extremely important to receive spiritual education from a young age at home.

To tell you specifically when I felt a longing for Buddha and God during such a childhood, I felt the presence of Buddha and God through my aspiration for self-improvement. Ever since I was relatively young, I remember having a powerful sense of mission and thinking there was something I had to do. At that age, I had no idea what that "something" was, but I had a strong determination to achieve something meaningful. I felt there was something I had to accomplish, even if it meant devoting or sacrificing everything that was dear to me. I think I looked for what that could be for decades.

There is a short novel called *Beyond the Pale of Vengeance*, by Kan Kikuchi. This story illustrates the life of a monk who devotes himself to digging a tunnel through a mountain. I, too, had the desire to accomplish a difficult task that would take decades to complete, and was in search for something that would engage my unyielding will. I wished ardently to live like the monk in the story, who devoted his life to digging Ao-no-Domon (Carved Tunnel of Ao) so that the villagers could travel more safely. When I was still an elementary school student, I was strongly drawn to the idea of devoting every spare moment to doing something worthwhile. Even as a child, I would sometimes look at an unabridged dictionary and strongly desire to create something equally great in the future.

In any case, the various thoughts and dreams that crossed my mind all had one thing in common: It was my desire to devote my entire life, not just a month or half a year but a decades-long timeframe of even 30 or 40 years, to doing work to achieve something of value. I wanted to create something great and, if possible, work on something that would benefit a large number of people far into the future. This feeling—this sense of mission—would well up powerfully from the depths of my heart.

Looking back today, I feel that the sense of mission I had from my childhood was actually my deep longing for Buddha and God. I believe that having a strong sense of mission was, after all, one kind of proof that the angels of light are born on Earth.

2

Memories of My Father

When thinking about family environments during one's childhood, I recall two examples that have impressed me. One example is John Stuart Mill (1806–1873), a British philosopher who developed the theory of utilitarianism. He was a student of Jeremy Bentham and a liberal economist. Mill described his childhood family environment in *The Autobiography of John Stuart Mill*, which is a masterpiece in autobiographical literature, so many of you may have read it.

Mill's father was a prominent scholar and a close friend of Bentham. From a very young age, Mill received special education from his father, and he was already able to read Greek, Latin, and numerous other difficult books in his primary school days. This man of genius also received much influence from his family environment.

But unfortunately, his intellectual and spiritual disposition reached a limit and stagnated after the age of 20, perhaps because he received such an advanced education from such a young age. Receiving an advanced education too early may have somehow worked to distort his will to conquer the weak self and his aspiration for self-improvement. Nevertheless, when I read his autobiography as a young adult, I was quite envious of the exceptional education his father had given him.

The other example is Hideki Yukawa (1907–1981), a Japanese theoretical physicist. He also recalls his upbringing in his autobiography, *Tabibito (The Traveler)*. Hideki Yukawa was from the Ogawa family, which was a family of prominent scholars. His father, Takuji Ogawa, was a professor at Kyoto University specializing in geology, and his brothers Tamaki Ogawa and Shigeki Kaizuka were also notable scholars. Hideki Yukawa went on to receive a Nobel Prize for physics.

Under the influence of his father and grandfather, Hideki Yukawa also received special education; from a young age, he was instructed to read aloud the Four Books and Five Classics of Confucianism. It is likely that this kind of diligent learning and spiritual influence during childhood served greatly in creating a genius in the future.

To some extent, I, too, had a similar experience, and I now recall it with great pleasure. My father was a very spiritual person. In his later years, he worked as an advisor to Happy Science (and later as Honorary Advisor) under the name Saburo Yoshikawa, and he also published some books. The name Saburo Yoshikawa was created by combining the Chinese characters taken from his names in his past and current lives: two characters from Zenmui-Sanzo (Subhakarasimha), one from Nichiro who was one of the six senior disciples of Nichiren, and one character from his name in this lifetime. He worked under this religious name.

The influence I received from my father in my youth was immense; I would not have been able to encounter Buddha and God so early if it had not been for him. My father did not have such a large collection of books, but since my primary school days, I had the impression that he was a person who thought deeply on matters and read things thoroughly. It was probably this image of my father that prompted me to develop my aspiration for self-improvement and my will to conquer the weak self.

My father did not have that many books on his shelf, but all the books were quite worn. One of the books I remember particularly well was the Bible. Both the Old and New Testaments were so worn out that they were losing shape. There were notes written everywhere, and many passages were underlined in red. I assumed it had been read numerous times over a few decades. Even as a young boy, I could tell that he had studied it very hard.

Something that impressed me the most about my father was his excellent memory. He would not just read the Bible, but could also freely recite the important passages from both the Old and New Testaments from memory. He often spoke to me about Bible verses, and he was also well versed in Zen Buddhism. One of the most important teachings of Zen is *The Gateless Gate*, and I heard my father lecture on it when I was only about 10 years old. So, by the time I was about 9 or 10, I was taught about the stories in the Bible and lectured on *The Gateless Gate* at home.

In his late teens, my father studied with Tadao Yanaihara's Non-Church Movement, but he later found the Christian teachings to be unsatisfactory and became a member of another religious group, Seicho-no-Ie, where he studied the philosophy of the monism of God. I learned that he also studied directly under the founder, Masaharu Taniguchi, shortly after World War II. Interestingly, even as he was studying the teachings of Seicho-no-Ie in his 20s, he was also involved in political activities and supported communist ideas.

I still find this odd, but apparently in his earlier years, my father managed to integrate, in his own unique way, the ideas of materialistic political reform and the monism of God, a philosophy that teaches that "there are essentially no material objects, nor any physical bodies." When thinking about why he was attracted to these mutually opposing beliefs, I now understand that the idea of creating a utopia from Karl Marx's teachings and Seicho-no-Ie's idea that "essentially there are only spirits; only God exists" were somehow connected in his mind, though not in a fully organized way.

As a result of my father's influence, I had an understanding of materialism since I was in primary school. I also learned about the contents of *The Communist Manifesto* by listening to my father. Besides these, my father also had books on the history of Western philosophy. There were not many of them, but I could tell that my father had read them over and over. He also spoke to me about Western philosophy.

I think I was about 10 or 11 when I first heard about Immanuel Kant. My father taught me about Kant's philosophy of idealism when I was in my final years of primary school. This of course was not a proper lecture, but every day after our evening meal, he would talk to my brother and me on the subject for an hour or so. My mother, who was not very well-read, seemed to have trouble understanding what my father said at times. But knowing that these talks were one of his greatest pleasures, she would quickly hide herself in the kitchen after the meal, and listen to our father talking to us through the door.

I have other memories of my father. I remember him always writing novels in his notebook on weekends. Our house was not very big, so every time he wrote, he would set up a small, low desk in one corner of the house and work on his novel. I also recall him composing haiku poems in the living room after we children had gone to bed. Apparently, he was very skilled at writing haikus, and when he submitted his work in competitions sponsored by national newspapers such as *Asahi Shimbun*, he often won first prize. I heard that some of his works were also introduced in "Saijiki," a special book of haiku.

Under his influence, I too developed an inclination for literature without realizing it and wrote poems. While I did not have a direct master of the Truth, I believe watching my father while growing up was the greatest lesson for me.

3

The Spirit of Conquering the Weak Self

I was brought up in such a family environment, and so it was natural for me to gradually develop a spirit of conquering the weak self. You can imagine the level of learning children do at school in the third, fourth, and fifth grades; their studies are not particularly difficult. But during those years, I learned about the philosophy of Kant, the ideologies of Marx and Engels, Wumen Huikai's *The Gateless Gate*, and the words of Jesus and the prophets of the Old Testament. These lessons were on a completely different level; even as a small child, I could understand the gap between what I learned at school and the actual Truth.

In those times, I used to think, "This kind of material is too advanced for a primary school child, and such studies are not suitable for me at this age. So, all I can do now is to do my best in studying the materials given to me as they come, while retaining the aspiration to learn these subjects in greater depth when I get older. I can only strive to improve myself in this way." In some ways, I could foresee the kind of person I would be 10 years in the future since that age.

So, for the next decade, I studied hard in my own way to get into university. During all that time, I would tell myself to study hard and build a foundation so that I could be worthy of learning the kind of philosophies, ideologies, and religions my father had taught me in my childhood. Then, from around the age of 20, I finally entered the world for which I had been preparing myself—the world of true learning. Upon entering university, I became deeply absorbed in reading different kinds of books. Naturally, most of the books were on ideology and philosophy.

As I look back on my younger days, I feel the spirit of conquering the weak self is extremely important for humans. People are apt to be drawn toward the easy path, allowing themselves to drift in everyday mundane life, but what prevents us from doing so is the will to triumph over our weaknesses. It is very important to have a desire to constantly improve oneself, even a little. It is also important to always be willing to study something of value and pass it on to others.

I believe that being able to maintain the willingness to learn or having an enthusiasm for learning is, in and of itself, a great talent. Some people have very shallow intellectual cravings and quickly become satisfied after learning very little, but there are also people who cannot be satisfied with little knowledge and are eager to go on to study further. I believe this kind of inclination or drive is itself a talent.

Perhaps many of you might complain, "Although I make efforts to the best of my ability, I cannot produce good results; my scores do not really go up, and I am hopeless at exams," or "No matter how hard I try at work, my efforts are not necessarily rewarded." However, the strong desire to learn something is already a talent. If you have this desire, or a strong wish to improve yourself, it will work as a driving force for you to leave the ordinary behind and head toward the extraordinary.

What matters is the level at which you feel satisfied. The less satisfied you feel or the further away you are from fulfillment, the stronger your will to conquer the weak self will be and the higher the "mountain peaks" you will climb. I have had this belief throughout my life, and because I had a high threshold for being satisfied, I could never get complacent about my intellectual ability. I would consistently set high goals for myself, so no matter my efforts, I was always far from achieving them.

In this sense, viewing life as an endless quest for self-improvement may be considered dangerous from the perspective of the philosophies of Lao-tzu and Chuang-tzu. However, we humans innately have the desire to live our lives to the fullest and to do the best work we can for as many people as possible because we are only born into this world once every few hundred or few thousand years. From this perspective, it would only be natural for us to aim for endless improvement.

The spirit of conquering the weak self is indispensable for someone starting out from the ordinary to reach an extraordinary height. Without it, it is impossible to attain self-realization in the truest sense. Having the spirit of conquering the weak self means you neither underestimate nor overestimate your abilities, but maintain the attitude of looking one step ahead and pushing yourself to reach a slightly higher goal. The majority of people fail to look ahead because they are content with the status quo. However, if they can just stretch themselves a little to look ahead, they will be able to get a view of what lies one step further and realize what it is they need to do.

Therefore, the driving force to nurture the spirit of conquering the weak self is the attitude of looking one step ahead. People tend to feel satisfied by focusing solely on their current situation, but if they maintain the attitude of looking one step ahead even if they have to push themselves a little, they will have a clearer idea of which direction to move toward and which areas to put more effort into.

4

Spiritual Views of Life

Growing up in such a childhood family environment, I gradually deepened my spiritual views of life. Even so, I could not help being intrigued by earthly matters. During adolescence in particular, I began to admire the opposite sex. I would imagine various ideals and be absorbed in various thoughts and contemplation.

In order to experience a religious awakening, there is one innate quality one absolutely needs, especially during the ages from about 17 to 23. It is how much one is able to look at the world as an ideal place. This is the prerequisite for awakening to religious Truth. I think one's feeling toward the opposite sex is a simple way to test this ability. How much one can admire someone of the opposite sex during adolescence will serve to be a source of great happiness for one's soul.

I regret that young people today have less admiration for the opposite sex and often seem to see or deal with them only to satisfy their own curiosity. But the extent to which you are able to admire the opposite sex with a pure heart during your adolescence will be a powerful influence later in life. Your inclination or the tendency of your mind to admire the opposite sex will eventually help you imagine and anticipate the ideal character in yourself and in others.

These years are the period of abundant dreams and ideals, but ironically, they are also a time for one to experience a setback or two. I, too, suffered a few setbacks during this period. During such times, the more idealistic you are or the loftier the ideals you have, the greater the shock you will suffer; it will feel as if you have fallen from the top of a cliff. People experience deep sorrow during these times when their souls are the purest and their hearts are the most innocent.

I believe one needs to experience sorrow at least once to attain a spiritual view of life. I do not necessarily suggest that you purposely seek out sorrowful experiences, but I must say that those who have never shed tears of regret from confronting failure or distress will not be able to know Buddha or God in the truest sense. It would be quite difficult for people who have never thought deeply about themselves in this way to know spirits, Buddha, or God.

In most cases, the cause or source of sorrow lies in the gap between one's ideals and reality. The greater the gap, the deeper the distress, pain, and sorrow the youth will feel. Still, it seems to me that sadness works like sandpaper or a whetstone that polishes one's soul in some way.

Some religious leaders boldly teach that there is no sadness or suffering in heaven, but to me, they only see half of life's truth. When thinking about why there is so much suffering and sorrow in life, we can see that such suffering serves as a kind of sandpaper to make the true colors of our souls shine even more beautifully. In a mundane, uneventful life, you will have less opportunity to reflect deeply on your mind. In such a life, you cannot know Buddha or God in the truest sense.

Among Christians, there are many who have suffered some kind of serious illness. While I do not recommend becoming sick, it is true that many feel Buddha or God close by for the first time after wandering at the edge of life and death. These experiences are actually thoroughly calculated; they are the rewards prepared by Buddha or God.

Buddha or God wishes humans to experience as many lessons as possible and gain as much nourishment for their souls from their one unique life of several decades. This is the truth, so rather than wishing for our lives to remain uneventful, we should feel grateful for being able to live through numerous hardships in different kinds of environments.

One's spiritual views of life will shine more beautifully as one undergoes experiences of sorrow and suffering. In the same way that a strong sword is created by beating red-hot iron with a hammer and quenching it in water, people are tempered by suffering and sorrow. Even among people who live cheerfully, there is an indescribable air and look of greatness in those who have experienced suffering or sorrow in life and have managed to overcome it. They are not simply cheery; they have developed a strong soul after fully experiencing the negative sides of life and nevertheless returning to the brighter world. That is how I perceive them.

5

Communicating with the Spirit World

After having gone through the sensitive years of adolescence, I started to communicate with the spirit world at the age of 24. As described in *The Laws of the Sun* (New York: IRH Press, 2018), this experience marked a great turning point that truly changed my life.

A few years before I began communicating with the spirit world, I had struggled greatly within my soul and experienced spiritual conflict. I reflected deeply on myself and shed bitter tears about how I had lived. I wept, thinking, "Why am I living based on a 'false self,' driven by vanity? I used to have pure ideals, but look how pretentious I have become. I have been putting on a brave front and letting pride control me without even realizing it. I constantly seek approval from others, but how did I come to have such mistaken thoughts and find myself mired in such a deep sense of failure?" I would reflect on my life deeply in this way and feel remorse.

I had started out in life with the awareness of being ordinary. But instead of advancing steadily and straightforwardly toward self-improvement, I would agonize over the gap between my ideals and reality. I was plunged once again into the mundane, which made me see just how ordinary I was. It came as a huge shock to me. At that time, I think I was being tested on whether I could stand up with an indomitable spirit again.

In my early 20s, I was in a dilemma of wanting to change the negative aspects of my character but being unable to do so completely. I was distressed by the unbridgeable gap between the ideal image I had of myself and who I was in reality. Based on the spirit of conquering the weak self I had cultivated from childhood, I believed those who worked hard must always be rewarded appropriately, and that people should achieve results worthy of their efforts. However, after several instances in certain areas of my life, I came to realize that there are times when one's efforts are not necessarily rewarded.

One of these areas was interpersonal relationships. At school, for example, if you study hard, your efforts are rewarded, but in personal relationships, efforts do not always yield good results. I experienced this profoundly. As a naive young man who was brought up in the countryside, I was attracted to a city girl. But when I found out that my efforts to seek her favor did not result in a desirable outcome, I fell into deep despair.

I later realized that with regard to personal relationships, there are many situations in which one cannot produce the desired results through effort alone. I ultimately discovered it is actually impossible to control other people's minds.

One of the pains of human experience, or suffering in life, springs from our desire to control the hearts of others to make them as we would like. We want others to think of us and treat us the way we wish. We naturally want things to be this way, but are unable to achieve it. It seems to me that people create suffering at such times.

I have seen numerous examples of this and have had these sorts of experiences myself. I have also encountered the suffering of many people through my current work of spreading the Truth. In the process, I have felt keenly that this issue must be considered from a different, deeper perspective.

The truth is that it is difficult to change other people's feelings. Everyone is granted the freedom of will; they are free to harbor any thought and act based on it. This is an individual right over which each person has full authority. We can have influence over others and provide materials or opportunities that may prompt them to change, but in the end, it is fundamentally up to each individual to change his or her mind. After I started communicating with the spirit world, this truth became even clearer to me as I experienced the other world and spoke with many different spirits.

I used to have a simple question about why hell should exist and why there should be such beings as evil spirits and devils. I would ponder time and again, "If God is Light and is an all-knowing and an all-powerful Being, and if the angels of light are so powerful, why is it that they cannot save evil spirits? Why can't they help all the devils out of hell?" However, when I looked deeply into the "minds," of both others and myself, I understood clearly why this was the case.

In fact, even though the angels of light can admonish the spirits in hell and the evil spirits, or provide them with materials to awaken to the Truth, they cannot forcibly change the minds of these spirits. Only the spirits themselves can change their own minds. I clearly understood this. No matter how much helpful material others provide a person, the one to change his or her mind, the protagonist of one's life story, is that person alone. We can only change our own minds. I came to know this to be an absolute law that flows throughout the entire universe.

Some people may see it as giving up or resignation, but I see a much more positive side to it. The question is whether or not you stop after discovering that you cannot control the minds of other people. We just saw that it is impossible to change another person's mind because everyone has the will to make decisions on their own. As long as this is true, the next step is for you to realize that you are capable of changing your own mind which suffers from not being able to change the minds of others.

I deepened my thoughts on this matter in the following way: "Before I worry about my inability to change others' minds, what about mine? Can I change my own mind? Am I able to rule and control it? First, I must strive to take control of myself and govern my own mind. If my mind is uncontrolled like a flooding river, breaking levees and damaging the surrounding fields, how can I tell others to control their minds to let it flow straight? Can I ever calm the river of my own mind?"

I realized how foolish we humans are to be frustrated by trying to change other people's minds, when in fact we cannot even control our own minds. And I felt how important it is to have 100 percent control of our own minds, to govern them completely. I then decided to put my efforts into consciously, intentionally, and willingly controlling my own mind and to build myself in this way.

Please remember that the first step is to have the will to control one's mind. Even if someone's heart does not turn to you or others do not say things you wish them to, before grieving over it, ask yourself if you can ease your own mind. If you cannot change or govern your own mind, how can you expect to change or control the minds of others?

There are countless people in the world who wish to be loved by others or to be loved by a particular person. There are also many people who create suffering because they cannot receive the love they desire. Then, how about your heart? When you look inside your heart, how much love do you have for others? You may like a particular group of people, but there are probably many whom you dislike. The people you dislike may be seeking your love, but since the direction in which you express your love does not change, this may become the source of their suffering. If so, you need to start by changing your inner self. This idea was my starting point.

Shakyamuni Buddha's teachings also started from the same idea. The very first starting points of Buddhism were how to find peace of mind, how to control the mind, and how to transcend all the emotions of joy, anger, sorrow, and pleasure to achieve the state of liberation. Shakyamuni Buddha always contemplated, "We humans tend to be swept along at the mercy of our emotions. Our minds are swayed by joy, anger, sorrow, and pleasure, and are constantly shaken up and down and swayed side to side. With such fluctuations, how can we find our own permanent self, an unchanging self, an unshakable self? How can we enter the Middle Way and attain a stable mind?"

He then came to the realization that "Pleasure that is sought from external sources is empty. The effort of searching for the cause of enlightenment or seeds of happiness outside ourselves will be in vain. So, look inside. Plant seeds in the field of your mind. Cultivate the field of your own mind." This was the starting point of Shakyamuni Buddha's enlightenment. Shakyamuni Buddha then went on to teach how to control one's mind from different angles. The Eightfold Path is one such teaching, and the Six Paramitas are another. Thus, I became keenly aware of the fact that I returned to the starting point of Buddhism through my own experience.

6

The Conflict between the Truth and Business

Around the same time I started communicating with the spirit world, I also began work at a Japanese trading house. I experienced these unique worlds of the trading business and the spiritual world simultaneously. On weekends or in the evenings on a weekday, I would open the window of my heart and contact a variety of spirits. Sometimes I even conversed with evil spirits. At the same time, I worked as a businessman and engaged in the import and export of goods between countries during the day. It was truly a strange feeling, and my soul was greatly trained during these years.

The world of international trade is a dog-eat-dog world, though maybe not as fierce as that of brokerage firms. My daily work was extremely rough; to keep up with the pace of work, I had to shift my focus with each passing moment, make decisions and take actions without a moment to lose. English was used everywhere in the office, on telephone calls and in documentation; I could not lose focus even for a minute.

As I worked in such an office environment, I eventually started to experience a recurring inner conflict between the contemplative side of me who wished to enter into deep meditation and explore the world of the mind, and the side who wished to express my full potential and succeed in the business world. It took three to four years before I finally reached a point where I could reconcile my business world self and Truth-exploring self to a certain degree.

During those years, my ideal image of myself did not coincide with reality and was not firmly set. There was too much of a gap between the me who was being trained in the social world and the me who was exploring the Truth, and I was unable to bridge this gap. Nevertheless, having harsh experiences and struggling with various relationships, I started to see and understand many things in my own way. My inner eye, or the eye of my mind, started to open, and at the same time, my view of the outer world also became clearer.

Working at the trading company, I was able to thoroughly explore the causes of suffering of people in business, the origin of distortions in human society, the reason why emotions give rise to conflict, and the reason people seek promotion, social status, and money. When I was sent abroad to work, I learned the ways of thinking of people from other countries as well.

Something else I gained from my experience in a trading house was to have different points of view. People working in a trading company look at things from an international perspective, so one must sometimes detach oneself from one's own nationality to view things from a foreign client's position. For instance, an export business in Japan would have a respective import business in the United States. The whole situation is seen from opposite ends; although one method may be considered best for exporting, the same method would have an opposite effect on the importing side. I had many of these kinds of experiences.

I believe these experiences of looking at things from a different or opposing standpoint and observing Japan and Japanese people from a foreigner's viewpoint or from the eyes of those with different upbringings had a significant influence on me in later years. It allowed me to discover new perspectives.

In practicing self-reflection, one needs to look at oneself from the eyes of a third party, but many people seem to have trouble understanding what is meant by an impartial third party. My experiences observing Japanese lifestyles and workstyles from an objective third-party position in a global setting provided me with new ideas to contemplate. I observed Japanese people and the Japanese way of working through the eyes and from the standpoint of foreigners. This later led me to understand how to self-reflect and how one should look at oneself objectively. These were truly profound experiences.

CHAPTER FIVE

Existence and Time

1

What is Existence?

This chapter introduces my thought on "existence," which represents one of my core philosophies. This is because all philosophical discoveries and findings of the Truth in this three-dimensional earthly world arise from one's way of understanding, observing, and interpreting "existence." If you open your eyes and look at the world around you, you can see that many things exist. Will you view those things haphazardly and accept them without going into deeper exploration, or will you try to grasp what lies at the heart of these existences? Herein lies an indicator that reveals the essence of a person's life.

There is a significant difference between those who perceive all existence as mere "existence," which has an external appearance and exists separately from themselves, and those who consider the meaning of all that exists and what it is that allows them to exist. Those who have explored the meaning of "existence" and have been able to successfully clarify its meaning are called the "awakened ones."

In today's society, religion, philosophy, and ideology are considered separately and are established as different subjects of study, but in truth, they all stem from a single act. Everything started from the act of exploring how to view the world, how to view the self that exists in the world, and how to give meaning to and interpret the world and the self.

This is also true of Buddhism. Buddhism places great importance on the Law of Cause and Effect. For something to exist, it must have a cause. Because there is a cause, there is an effect. For something to appear, there are a few different kinds of causes. As a result of these causes, some phenomena will arise without fail. Therefore, if the phenomenon you encounter is bad, you must first correct the cause. Regarding the causes of the past, practice self-reflection to remove the bad seeds. Regarding the future, prevent yourself from planting seeds that would yield bad phenomena. This is the core idea of the Law of Cause and Effect.

Now, calm your mind and reflect on yourself. What kind of existence are you?

There are many people who lead busy lives every day, and many of you may also be living in such a way. I am sure you have pondered over your existence at least a few times. But you may have long forgotten the question or the issue without having reached an answer. Perhaps you are too preoccupied with trying to find an explanation for the current phenomena or the events happening around you right now.

If you work for a company, for example, you may consider it a matter of course to work there and simply focus on how to do your job, how to earn the praise of others, or how to spend your earnings. You may be content with experiencing various things as they happen. However, you must realize that asking fundamental questions like, "What am I doing? What is the purpose of my life? Where did I come from and where will I go?" is by no means a special right granted only to the youth.

Even if you had questions about where you had come from, where you would go, or who you really are at some point during your high school or university days, you probably have long forgotten these questions and have allowed yourself to get lost in everyday busyness. However, have you ever considered how wasteful life would be if you were to live without knowing who you truly are, where you came from and where you will go, or the true nature of the world?

Look at all the creatures and materials that exist in this world, and think about the meaning of their existence. Start by asking yourself this question: Why do they exist?

Why do people exist? Why do plants and flowers exist? Why do animals exist? Why do humans need to eat food? Why are humans born? Why do people become sick? Why do we grow old? Why do we all die? And what happens to us after death?

What about the world? Why does Earth rotate once every 24 hours? Why does Earth orbit the Sun as it rotates on its own axis? Why does the Sun continue to radiate heat and light in that way?

Do spirits truly exist? What will happen if they do exist? And if God really exists, how does God see me now?

These are the questions I want you to ponder. I believe questioning these issues is the starting point and a requirement of being human.

God gave humans the power of thought, the ability to think. Without using this power to think deeply over the significance and the meaning of existence, I do not think there is a point in being born in this lifetime. You may be imagining in your mind that spirits exist and God exists, but perhaps you are afraid of exploring this deeply.

Now, look at yourself on the assumption that God exists. How would you appear in God's eyes? How would God see you? How do you think God sees Earth? How do you think God sees this world? And why did God create man and woman? If you accept that spirits exist, that spirits are the essence of humans, and that spirits reside in physical bodies to live an earthly life, then surely your views of life will change. You will then realize you have been losing sight of your true self. Please consider these points.

2

The Origin of Existence

I have posed several questions about "existence." Let us think about what lies at the origin of people, material objects, air, the sun, water, and other things that exist in this world. Many people have come up with different answers for the reason of existence; some claimed that the world was comprised of the fundamental elements of earth, water, fire, and air, while others considered that everything was made of ether. However, as a result of my continual research, I have found that there is an undeniable law that states, "Thoughts take concrete form and manifest externally."

Even on Earth, it is possible to create something if you wish to create it and work hard on it. In the same way that you can create clay figures, if you decide to form a company, start a business, build an airplane or a ship, or produce a computer, these thoughts will manifest themselves through effort. What appears in this way is merely an earthly phenomenon. But how did humans, who have such thoughts, come into being in the first place? How did all the materials used to create things appear? How did this vast land come to be? How did human beings emerge? Did we really evolve from amoebas? There are endless questions to ponder.

I, too, contemplated many things in my exploration of the origin of existence. I thought about the matter thoroughly, and with various experiences, came to a single answer: "The origin of all existence is one Will. There was a Will that let everything be. The three-dimensional world we live in is the physical embodiment of this Will." The reason this three-dimensional world exists is because there is unquestionably a power that allows it to be.

Humans exist and are alive because there is a Will that commands, "Humans, be." It means there is a Will that wishes to create human beings. Without this Will, humans would never exist. In concrete terms, parents give birth to babies, whose bodies develop from the intake of earthly food. But before that can happen, there are bodily functions necessary to create children. What mandates these functions is the functioning of the mind, and God's Will is what creates this mental function.

God, an existence at the very depth of the other-dimensional world, created the multi-dimensional realm extending from the fourth dimension and higher. That same Will created this unique three-dimensional materialized world, and it contains the Will that allows humans to be.

If the nature of this Will changed, it might not be impossible for humans to give birth to animals and for animals to give birth to humans. But the reason morning glory seeds eventually bloom as morning glory flowers is because there is a Will that thinks well of such flowers blooming and because there is a great life energy that supports that Will. This is all in accordance with the Will of God. For those who have experienced the worlds beyond this earthly world in the fourth dimension and higher, this is an undeniable fact.

Moreover, the law stating that "One's thoughts instantly become actions, and one's actions immediately manifest into results" is common knowledge for those who have passed on to inhabit the other world as spirits. These spirits know that even though they are not God, they can create the world through their will; they can change their own images and create various objects using their will. They have actually experienced this.

As evidence of their experiences, I have published numerous books of spiritual messages and interviews. Various spirits send me spiritual messages, which are then transcribed into books. These books are the materialization of their ideas into three-dimensional form, but these ideas were originally found in the fourth dimension and above. These philosophies, which shine brilliantly in the worlds beyond the fourth dimension, are translated into three-dimensional terms to be published in the form of a book.

Once we know this truth, we cannot ignore the solemn law that "Thoughts take shape and manifest themselves." To put it another way, the origin of existence is a will, and the origin of that will is the Will of God. It is the Will of God that created individual life forms, and these life forms created other new things, following the Will of God. This is the secret to the history of the creation of this Earth and the universe. I have finally discovered this truth by investigating and exploring the world of spirits in many ways.

This world is indeed the world of thoughts. In the Bible, there is a phrase: "In the beginning was the Word, and the Word was with God, and the Word was God." "Word" here can be replaced by "Will," and the phrase can be read, "In the beginning was the Will, and the Will was with God, and the Will was God." In other words, God is Will and God's Will created everything. As the result of this Will, God spoke the Words. This is the Truth.

3

The Miracle of Love

In exploring the meaning and origin of existence, I cannot help but feel that there is a great miracle involved. I can only believe that there is a miracle—something that lies beyond earthly perception.

People in this world are becoming more skeptical now, but the spirit world exists 100 percent. I can guarantee it. Nevertheless, many people in the world are overly fearful of being deceived. In truth, even those who study religion are unwilling to believe the words of others. This is because they are trying to interpret the world in terms of their own ego or false self. However, such resistance means that they believe they can understand everything with their own limited perception. I can only say that they have forgotten the fact that the spiritual world and the three-dimensional world, which is a reflection of the spiritual world, came into existence as a result of the miracle of God's love.

God is great love. God has created all things with this great love. The driving force of God's expression of His Will is love. Love is God's wish for all beings to be good, to prosper, and to be happy. Such Will has been realized and has manifested itself in reality in different ways.

When thinking about this world, you need to be aware that love lies at its depths, and that love is the power which makes miracles happen. Love gives rise to such great power. Anyone can confirm this miraculous power of love; it is evident in how people can overcome any difficulty with love, even on Earth.

I feel my existence most keenly when I sense the presence of love. When I feel love in myself and around me, I immediately understand the reason why I exist, why the world exists, why other people exist, and why plants and animals exist. I understand these things almost instantaneously. The secret key to understanding the meaning of existence and the meaning of the existence of the world is to know love. If you look at existence from the perspective of love, you will find a secret there.

Think about human beings from the perspective of love. Think about yourself from the perspective of love. Your existence originated from the love of your parents, who were also created by God. You exist today because of God's love. What is more, as proof that God loves you, you have been given everything you need.

What a blessing it is to have other people around you. How many people in the world feel grateful for the existence of others? You must understand that the very existence of other people is an expression of love for you. Because other people exist and come together to create societies, you are able to work, to find a reason to live for, and to express yourself. You cannot express yourself if you are all alone in this world. You can only do so when there are many other existences, including other people, and the world and environment that allow these people to exist.

Imagine what kind of work there would be if you existed all by yourself in a faraway place in the great universe, floating all alone in a vacuum. What kind of self-realization would there be in that condition? What kinds of efforts would you be able to make? What kind of self-awareness could you possibly have? As you think of these things, you will come to realize that the existence of other people is love itself.

Here is the worldview you must now have: You yourself are an existence of love, and so are those around you. In the world of love, you exist as an expression of love. Love attracts love, and together, they strive to create future visions of a new world. You are currently living in this kind of miraculous space.

In fact, love is the reason for all existence. Why is there a desk? Surely, that is also an expression of love. It is a manifestation of someone's wish to benefit others. Why is there an egg? Why is there bread to eat? Why is there air? Why is there water? Why are there things to drink? Why is there a bed to sleep on? These are all manifestations of love. We must know that we are wrapped in the soft feathers of love. The miracle of love—that is the source of all existence. You need to start afresh with this view of the world in mind.

4

Time: The Motion of Existence

I have talked about how all that exists in this world is an expression of love and how everything is a manifestation of love. I have also described love as the reason for existence—the power that allows all to exist. Now, I would like to touch on the subject of time because the concept of time is also a key to unlocking the secret of life and the meaning of human existence.

In this three-dimensional world, we need to understand the world from the perspectives of both existence and time. If time did not exist, all three-dimensional activity would stop, just like a frozen screen. But what would this mean? It would mean that people would be no different from the mannequins we see in shop windows. Can you consider this to be the true world?

What would appear if all movements suddenly halted, if Earth stopped rotating, if people stopped moving, if the air stopped circulating, if water stopped flowing, and if the sun stopped radiating heat and energy? There would no longer be existence, and everything would simply be images on a screen—mere shadows of reality. There would be nothing more than images or scenes of the past shown on film.

Imagine Earth or the whole universe to be motionless. Suppose that right now, as you are reading this book, time stopped. What would you or the world look like?

Neither knives nor bullets would be necessary to take your life. If time were to stop, your life would disappear because there would be no meaning to your existence. If the present time or era were frozen instantaneously, all meaning of existence would be lost. In fact, different eras exist, and people live and carry out various activities in each era, because time passes.

God is a great inventor, and among all of His inventions, time is probably the most precious. If God had not invented time, what would have been the consequence of the world He created? It would be a completely motionless world, a state of total silence with no movement. In such a world, some things would suddenly pop up while others would abruptly disappear; this world would be no more than a repetition of such appearances and disappearances. So, the invention of time was actually a great invention by God when the world was created. Coming up with the passage of time was the greatest revelation God had.

Before that, there was of course the revelation, or invention, of the power to create or manifest things through will. The truth is that "creating things through the power of will" and "shaping the world through time" are the two greatest inventions of God. God designed many things, but nothing is more important than these two inventions: the law of material manifestation and the law of time.

In other words, time was granted for beings to exist and move, and when existence was allowed motion, the history of humankind and the history of the universe began. What is more, because existence was given time and therefore motion, growth and development were guaranteed. If time did not exist, the world would be stationary; there would be no development and no change. From this perspective, I hope you will understand how the flow of time is a precious element that makes up the universe, and how significant this invention is.

5

The Essence of Time

Let us now consider more deeply the essence of time. For humans, time is measured by the movement of the hands on a clock, which move according to the speed of Earth's rotation on its axis and Earth's revolution around the Sun. From this, we can understand that time has a distinctive character; for Earth, there is "time on Earth."

If humanlike intellectual beings exist on another planet, I am sure their time would be different from that of Earth because time differs depending on the speed of a planet's rotation on its own axis and the speed of its revolution around a fixed star. If one day on their planet equaled one month on Earth, the inhabitants would probably be moving very slowly. On the contrary, if their month were equivalent to one day on Earth, the inhabitants would appear to be leading very busy lives, just as in a fast-forwarded animation.

When considering time, I must also mention that time has unique characteristics. You may think of time as being invariable, but the truth is that numerous forms of time exist in this great universe; time can have a different nature and its own distinctive characteristics. This is not only true of this earthly world, but also in the heavenly world; in heaven, time represents the speed of one's spiritual evolution.

When we talk of speed, or about something being "fast" or "slow," we often try to express it by assessing it in relative terms. But whether something is truly fast or slow depends on what it is being compared to, so it is impossible to determine whether things are fast or slow in absolute terms.

For example, the movement and growth of plants appear very slow to the human eye; in fact, plants do not appear to move at all. However, with time-lapse photography, we can see that plants also move just as animals do. The truth is that the movement of plants is extremely slow compared to the speed at which humans move, and that is why they appear to be still. In this way, it is important to know that time has diverse and distinctive characteristics.

While plants appear motionless from the perspective of humans, how would humans appear to them? From the perspective of plants, humans would probably seem to be moving at an extremely high speed. To them, humans would seem the same as a bullet train or a supersonic airliner passing at full speed in front of us.

From this we can say that in essence, time is neither invariable nor absolute. Time simply exists to allow existence to move, and depending on the movement of each being, time can be diverse and have its own distinctive characteristics. After all, time is an essential factor in materializing one's will; it represents the duration for one's will to take tangible form. The speed of time changes depending on will.

This is a fairly philosophical interpretation of time, and many people may find it difficult to understand. However, without a clear understanding of this concept of time, we cannot grasp the true understanding of the world. We must understand the importance of viewing the world from the perspective of time and the invention of time as God's great revelation.

In the same way that humans appear to be diverse and unique from the perspective of people, time, which flows throughout the universe, also appears diverse and unique in the eyes of the high spirits and God. Furthermore, even on Earth, time possesses different natures and characteristics and is diverse. Time is different for plants and for animals, and also for humans. There are different types of time in this way.

These different types of time manifest through the movement of each being, and the movement of every being is actually the manifestation of love. Ultimately, what constitutes time is the development of love, and the duration of love undergoing change is called "time." It can be summed up in this way.

6

Time Known as Life

To close this chapter, I would like to consider "life and time." In the end, people who have never looked at their lives afresh from the perspective of time will lose in life. Time on Earth is uniform when measured on a clock, but what if you look at your life from the perspective that everyone lives on his or her own unique time? You will be left with a shocking realization and an amazing truth. I truly wonder why this is not taught at school.

Many people believe that time is equally given to everyone. Indeed, all people equally have 24 hours in a day. However, the significance of time is completely different for each person, depending on that person's pace in life. If people knew the length of time they would have on Earth at the time of birth, their life would probably be quite different. The pace of life for someone who is given 80 years of life would probably differ from that of someone with 30 years or someone else who has 15 years. When you understand this, I am sure your way of life will change.

There was a man who compared life to gold coins and said, "Everyone is given gold coins; some have 80 gold coins, others 50, and yet others 30. It is each person's mission to think about how to spend these coins." This interpretation of life makes a good point. When considering how to live through one's unique time called "life," we cannot avoid thinking about our own unique time.

Everyone is living his or her own unique time; people live not only based on the time measured by a clock, but also the time that is given specifically to them. The latter sense of time can be viewed from two different perspectives. The time each person lives is actually comprised of two elements. One is "relative time," or time that can be measured against the time of other people. For instance, the time spent taking a one-hour class with others, or sleeping eight hours, is considered "relative time."

On the other hand, there is another criterion called "absolute time." There is almost an infinite disparity between the effectiveness of time used for something meaningful and the effectiveness of time used for something meaningless during one's life. "Absolute time" is based on this perspective. If we consider our time as gold coins, it is natural for there to be a difference depending on what the money was used for. If a person used his or her gold coins as capital to produce great work, he or she would gain positive results and be rewarded accordingly. But if someone used the coins for meaningless purposes and poured money down the drain, he or she would face negative consequences accordingly. Thus, "absolute time" is measured by the amount of time used for the causes that accord with the Will of God.

Each person's life would be quite different if it were measured from the perspective of "absolute time." Suppose two people had the same life span of 70 years on Earth. If one of them strove to live more of his lifetime in "absolute time" while the other simply spent his days in "relative time," the two would be living in totally different time systems and their overall achievements in life would be quite different. I hope you will use these two ways of looking at time to think about your life.

We all live in both "relative time" and "absolute time." "Relative time" is shared with others; it is time you spend doing various jobs just like other people and time necessary for your livelihood. On the other hand, "absolute time" is time you spend in connection to the Truth, and this can be expanded boundlessly. For instance, the one-hour sermon given by Shakyamuni Buddha is time which expands across 2,000 or 3,000 years. The hour spent listening to that sermon was probably equal to several thousand years' worth of study for the souls of the people who were there. The great secret to being triumphant in life is to increase the amount of "absolute time" in this way. Increase the amount of "absolute time," for this is ultimately the way to be victorious in life.

CHAPTER SIX

To the Extraordinary Heights of Love

1

An Introspective Feeling

This book mainly describes the inner struggles and mindset one needs to have to set out from the ordinary to reach the extraordinary. I have also described the origin of my thoughts and how those thoughts were formed in various sections.

Through tireless, turtle-like efforts, an ordinary person eventually heads toward the heights of enlightenment. Throughout this book, I have tried to indicate enlightenment and the path leading to its entrance from different angles. Although this is just a rudimentary discussion on enlightenment and only an invitation to its first steps, I am trying to show how someone who started from the ordinary can have limitless possibilities in attaining enlightenment.

Having been born into this world as a human, it is difficult to live the exact life you want to live. However, no matter your abilities, circumstances at birth, or the environment in which you were raised, there will always be a spiritual awakening fitting to your specific background, and the developmental stages of enlightenment best suited for your position. No matter which path you take, these stages of enlightenment will eventually lead you to God. This is an undeniable fact. Therefore, the most crucial factor is your mindset or mental attitude in pursuing enlightenment.

Enlightenment is very deep; it has a mystical, profound feeling to it and carries something that cannot be fully understood by human perception. I have continuously published many books on the Truth to clarify what enlightenment is, and as the first step toward enlightenment, I want you to value an introspective feeling.

Introspection means reflecting on one's inner self. Those who have never reflected upon their inner selves cannot take a spiritual leap. All philosophies, schools of thought, religions, and even the sciences in the truest sense, were born from introspective thinking. In truth, what has already been achieved or exists in the Real World is granted to people on Earth. In this sense, it is most important to reflect on one's inner self.

It was spring when I started to communicate with the spirit world at age 24. During the six months leading up to that point, I had been having very strong introspective feelings. I would experience a sense of deep remorse for my past and, at the same time, feel compassion toward all living beings.

For example, I was once touched deeply by the death of a single river fish, which came to me as an extremely emotional sensation. It was during my fourth year at university, during the autumn before my graduation. I loved to go fishing since I was a child, so I decided to go fishing at a river in my hometown after a long absence.

The life of a river fish is very fragile; I would put the fish I caught in my fishing basket, but by the time I was ready to go home, most of the fish were dead, with their silver bellies facing upward. Before leaving, I returned the dead, uneatable fish back into the river. On seeing the white belly of one of the fish floating downstream that day, I was greatly struck by the transience of life. And for some reason,

I have not gone fishing again since then. It is probably because the intrinsic sorrow of the deaths of those fish struck my heart.

While that experience was not the direct cause, around that time, I was deeply contemplative about my life. I would feel deep remorse about how I had hurt many people with my words, and I would recall various things as I reflected on my life since birth. I asked myself why I had said things to hurt others, why I had ignored the feelings of others and their kindnesses, and how I had come to harbor selfish emotions.

At first, I was seized by feelings of self-hatred, but eventually I was led to the innermost depths of profound self-reflection. I remember that as I looked very deeply into my inner self, my view of the world gradually changed for the first time.

From that time on, I became capable of looking at the world around me with an entirely different perspective. Up until then, I felt as if I had been looking at the world from inside a fishbowl, but suddenly, I was able to see everything with a fresh new feeling. I remember experiencing this change. There were still many unresolved matters within me, but I think this was the first step in the true battle against myself.

When I wished to be reborn and begin a new life after feeling disgust and hatred toward what I had become, my introspective feelings grew deeper. I think it was a stepping-stone for me to eventually become attuned to the spirit world later on. I certainly encountered and discovered the knowledge of the Truth between the time I started introspecting and the time I became attuned to the spirit world. I believe that the internal force of self-reflection and the external force of the knowledge of the Truth worked together to crack open the shell that had been covering my heart.

2

The Appearance of Nichiren

I can never forget what happened on the afternoon of March 23, 1981: A high spirit came down to me for the first time. The first contact took the form of automatic writing. I have outlined the details of this event in *The Laws of the Sun*.

On the afternoon of that day, I was seated at my legless chair, enjoying the warmth of the early spring sunshine. Suddenly, I felt an indescribable warmth welling up inside me and instinctively sensed that someone was trying to give me a message. I looked around for something to write on and picked up a card that lay beside my desk. As soon as I placed the card in front of me, a strange phenomenon occurred: My right hand picked up a pencil to write something on its own volition. My intuition was right; my hand began to move as if it belonged to someone else. It wrote the words, *"Iishirase, Iishirase"* (Good News, Good News) in Japanese *katakana* syllabary.

The first spiritual being that contacted me was actually the Japanese Buddhist monk named Nikko, one of six senior disciples of Nichiren. This was his first message. About a week to 10 days later, my communication with Nikko came to an end, and then Nichiren started to contact me. At first, he did not give me his real name. Instead, he used the name of one of his six senior disciples, but I soon figured out that it had in fact been Nichiren himself. Eventually, Nichiren started conversing with me on a daily basis.

Initially, the spiritual conversation took place mostly through automatic writing. This communication through automatic writing, in which my hand would write various things on its own volition, continued for quite some time. I think the automatic writing started at the end of March of 1981 and continued until about the beginning of July of the same year. Around that time, I sensed the possibility of communicating not only through writing but also through speech. I would occasionally experience different thoughts and hear "voiceless voices" popping up in my mind, so I felt that perhaps I might be able to talk with spirits. Then, it turned out that the spirits who had communicated with me by automatic writing could actually speak by using my vocal chords. In this way, I began having verbal discussions with the spirits, though to an onlooker it may have appeared as if I were talking to myself.

The first half of 1981 was a memorable and significant time for me because it was when I truly grasped the sense for spiritual matters. In my head, I had thought I already knew enough about the world after death and the spiritual world, but my life took a 180-degree turn when I actually gained the spiritual power to conduct automatic writing through my own hand and deliver spiritual messages through my own mouth.

The kind of spiritual training I underwent before gaining the ability to communicate with spirits was nothing special. At the very least, I did not meditate under a waterfall or in a cave, or seclude myself in the mountains. There was only one thing I did: I looked deeply into my mind and strove to correct any wrongs I found there. Upon thoroughly examining the 24 years of my life, I realized I had committed many mistakes, so I deeply repented them. I had unknowingly been preparing myself to open the window of my mind.

As I unintentionally continued to purify my mind, I came to attain the next stage of awareness; a strong sense of duty to live for the sake of many people welled up from the depths of my heart.

As I reflected on the first 24 years of my life, I felt I was in the wrong because I realized that I had only been thinking about myself, my benefit, and my own success and greatness to gain the respect and praise of others. When I realized this, I felt deeply ashamed. I asked myself, "How much have I done for the sake of others? How much have I helped others with a selfless heart?" and I strongly felt I had to change my ways.

I could say that at age 24, I experienced my first "death." It was a total "death." In other words, I buried the false self I had until that point. This is how I came to have a strong desire to live for the sake of others. I wanted to do something for others.

However, I was still in the first half of my 20s and had just taken my first steps as an adult member of society. Being such a young man, it was extremely difficult to realize my ideals, and even though I wanted to live for the sake of others, I did not know exactly what I had to do. I knew my true mission should not be limited to small acts of kindness. I had my own gifts and abilities, innate character, and personal experiences. My challenge was how to best use these elements to be of service to the world and to help other people, and it weighed heavily on my mind. Nevertheless, at the very least, this marked a turning point in my life; I felt grateful and desired to give back to others after looking back at my life and reflecting on my past thoughts and deeds.

It was at such a time that Nichiren appeared before me. At first, I could not understand why Nichiren came to me, so I presumed that I had been a student of the Nichiren sect of Buddhism in one of my past lives. But after communicating with Nichiren for some time, I learned that my father, Saburo Yoshikawa, had been one of his most beloved disciples in a past life, and that connection had led him to contact me. It was an unbelievable experience that drastically changed my views of life.

3

Love, Nurture, and Forgive Others

Nichiren communicated many different messages to me, sometimes through automatic writing and at other times through my voice. At the time, since I had no intention of publishing books or teaching others the knowledge I was given as I am doing now, most of the messages only concerned my personal matters.

I spoke with Nichiren at various times and places, including on my commute between home and work and during my lunch breaks. I could not speak out loud when riding the train, so I would generally communicate with him by writing with my finger. In places where I had no access to paper, I often conversed in the form of automatic writing using my finger.

As previously noted, the majority of the messages I received from Nichiren at the time mostly concerned my personal matters, but the one phrase I still remember very clearly was "Love, nurture, and forgive others." He sent me this message through automatic writing very early on. When I asked him what my mission was and where my future lay, he replied with the three concepts of loving, nurturing, and forgiving others. He then mentioned that these words would become the core of my philosophy, but did not go into further detail.

Nichiren also gave me the words "Believe in people, the world, and God." So, I deeply contemplated those two phrases, "Love, nurture, and forgive others," and "Believe in people, the world, and God." I think the first message is a teaching that everyone can understand.

I understood the second message in the following way: "Believe in people" means we must believe in the divine nature, or Buddha-nature, that is dormant in all people. We must believe that they are essentially children of God, and that all people have the divine nature within them as children of God. "Believe in the world" is the natural consequence of the belief in people's Buddha-nature. It means we must not look upon this world as evil, but as a world made up of the children of God and therefore a world that should be a utopian society. Even if it may not appear to be that way now, the ideal world existing in the Real World must essentially be realized on Earth. This is how we should perceive this world and our society. Furthermore, the phrase "believe in God" is the first and last message, and this is the starting point of faith.

My thoughts would mainly focus on the three concepts of "Love, nurture, and forgive others." I slept on this phrase for a long time, until it eventually came to fruition about six years later as "the developmental stages of love," which were described in *The Laws of the Sun*. I continued to contemplate over the three concepts again and again, and finally came to the realization that this phrase actually related to the developmental stages of love.

Traditionally, Buddhism has valued the stages of enlightenment, or the development of enlightenment. On the other hand, Christianity has placed great importance on love. Since the attitude of seeking enlightenment and the attitude of giving love to others are quite different, it was difficult to reconcile the two. I think this is the reason these two major religious thoughts have always been in conflict and would not come together. However, after letting the three concepts of "Love, nurture, and forgive others" rest and "ferment" for six years, I managed to bridge these two beliefs by sublimating it into "the developmental stages of love."

I realized that the first stage of human love is the kind of love you express to those you should love naturally, such as your parents, siblings, relatives, colleagues, and others you meet in the course of your life. I call this stage "fundamental love," which is, in a sense, the starting point of love for all people.

On the next level, there is a higher stage of love, which I named "nurturing love." As we observe the world, we see many so-called "leaders." But what on earth makes them leaders? The fact is that they all share the desire to nurture others; they make it a principle to act on a grander scale of love and a highly evolved form of love. Such types of people become leaders and guide others. Due to their position, leaders must love many people, beyond the ones they meet in life or the ones they should naturally love. They must give others the love known as "guidance." Such outstanding people exist. In this way, I came to the realization that such a higher level of love, called "nurturing love," exists.

I also discovered an even higher level of love, "forgiving love," which even excellent leaders cannot necessarily possess. This love is based on a religious standpoint. People who excel in the earthly world can take various actions to nurture others, but to reach the stage of forgiving love, they need to experience "great enlightenment." It is important for them to experience a religious awakening and attain the state of mind of God or Buddha. I realized that there is a higher stage of love that transcends the differences of good and evil, and "forgiving love" is the love of true religious leaders. Thus, this was the challenge that occupied my mind since my first contact with Nichiren.

4

Confronting the Devil

As I received various spiritual revelations from Nichiren and other high spirits, I was simultaneously kept very busy every day at work in the trading company. Despite having awakened to the first stage of enlightenment, my heart would waver many times in these circumstances. I started to develop new attachments, which included my desire to achieve self-realization at the company. I had the desire to win recognition from others, to be better than everyone else, and become one of the elite. This led me to create different kinds of suffering, and I felt deeply hurt when things at work repeatedly went against my expectations.

I also sensed barriers between myself and the people at work, like my superiors and my colleagues. This was something I had never felt as a student. This eventually gave rise to conflicting emotions in my mind. Although I had awakened to the loftiness of my divine nature, I came to realize that new employees and novice workers were all treated like servicemen or private soldiers in Japanese society. I started to have serious doubts about the world in a Japanese seniority system and the world that assesses the value of an employee by the number of years he or she has worked for a company. I was very frustrated by how people's worth was judged solely by the length of time they worked for a company, and not by the level of their soul, awareness, or enlightenment.

There would have been no problem if those who stood above others were truly great people, but there were actually many different types of people; there were those who deserved the respect of subordinates and those who did not. It was unbelievable to me that they were all treated equally despite this difference.

While it may be inappropriate to describe someone as a "good person" or a "bad person," there were actually people who were inclined toward good and those who were inclined toward evil from a spiritual perspective. It was a great surprise for me to find that the people who were inclined toward evil and the people with stronger egotistical, aggressive natures in the eyes of God and Buddha, or in light of the Truth, were rather favored in this world. So, I secretly began aspiring to create a workplace based on true values, according to the level of people's state of mind. I thought there was a need for this kind of company and organization, and for this kind of world.

However, as someone working as a "pawn" in one of the leading trading companies in contemporary Japan, I could hardly make it a reality. All I could do was to do good work and give as much love as possible to the people around me. I decided to treat many people with love, both openly and discreetly, not necessarily in a conspicuous manner but in an unperceivable manner. I was limited to such small acts of love at the time.

During this period, not only was I distressed by the discord among people at work, but I was also experiencing a yearning for someone of the opposite sex. Despite having opened the window of my mind to speak with high spirits, I found my thoughts wavering as I came across many women in society and recognized their beauty. My mind would become agitated, and I would spend days without being able to concentrate my mind.

When your mind wavers with desires for social status or the opposite sex, devils secretly approach you. And, much like other religious leaders of the past, I too had to eventually confront several devils. Among them were the historically famous devil Lucifer, who is said to be the ruler of hell, and Beelzebub, who tempted Jesus while he was fasting for 40 days and nights in the desert. These kinds of devils would appear before me one after the other. I was also confronted by a devil with powerful spiritual powers, who had made a name for himself as a monk of Japanese esoteric Buddhism in the school of thought of Kobo-Daishi Kukai. They successively made appearances to torture me.

They took advantage of my spiritual sensitivity; whenever I was in poor condition or my emotions were disturbed, they would say things to delude me and try to divert my mind from the Truth. Whenever I had some kind of attachment, they would amplify it so that my mind would be filled with thoughts of whatever I was attached to, and try to make me worry and obsess over it. My fatigue doubled and even tripled, and sometimes I was unable to sleep at night.

As those difficult days continued, I was eventually left with no other choice but to fight the devils. This was ultimately all due to the weaknesses of my mind. I came to realize that devils are not mere external existences, but creep into the weaknesses of one's mind and actually reside within the mind. In fact, they sneaked up to me because of my pride.

Having studied on my own in a small rural town, and having eventually moved to the capital, graduated from the University of Tokyo Faculty of Law, and joined a trading company, I had my own feelings of inferiority and other worries. Despite this, I was still considered to be among the elite from a worldly perspective. I had a desire to gain recognition in society, which also came with feelings of self-preservation—I wanted to flee from the Truth. I wanted to escape from the path of the Truth and from my special ability to receive spiritual messages. It was through these weaknesses of my mind that the devils entered.

They would whisper into my ears: "You will never be happy unless you stop communicating with the high spirits and abandon your willingness to teach the Truth to others. Once you abandon the Truth and enlightenment, and discard the idea of teaching others, you will be successful in society; you will be promoted at work, achieve good standing, earn a higher income, and find a beautiful woman to marry." They took advantage of my weaknesses in this way, using delusions and temptations, which are commonly used on someone who is about to attain enlightenment.

During this period, I had several painful experiences. But the one thing I stuck with even at such times was to concentrate on refining myself. I told myself, "I have no way of knowing what will happen in the future. No matter how impatient I get in achieving my goals, I cannot see what lies ahead of me. I still have no idea how to put the phrase 'Love, nurture, and forgive others' into practice. But, in time, I'm sure there will be a calling. The time for me to stand before the world will come. Until then, I can only work to develop myself.

"I will remain humble and work to refine myself. After all, I originally began from the ordinary. Maybe it was wrong for me to believe I was a great person just because I became attuned to the spirit world. I am just an ordinary person, so I will live as an ordinary citizen, a good citizen. I will live in a way so that I will be regarded as a respectable human being, even if my spiritual abilities are to be taken away or even if I didn't have them at all. I will make myself shine brilliantly while living an ordinary life." I made up my mind to think this way.

I then completely cast away the pride I had for possessing spiritual abilities and the belief that I was special because of them. I decided to be a good, admirable person to others, even if I abandoned all my spiritual abilities. I would be pleasant like a soft spring breeze, be someone people would feel glad to have known, and live as a good, ordinary citizen. In this way, I made up my mind to live by examining my way of living and reflecting on the points where I had been mistaken. Thus, I cast aside my spiritual qualities and started to reexamine myself with the goal of becoming a capable and pleasant person.

Then, I gradually began to triumph over the devils within. After I discovered a way of life that would allow me to give out light in the midst of ordinariness, the devils finally left me.

Devils take advantage of the unguarded areas that are formed in one's mind when one wants to be extraordinary. In particular, they creep into the weaknesses in the minds of people who are trying to become exceptional by seeking to gain spiritual abilities. What drove them away was neither a strong reprimand nor powerful spiritual abilities; it was my indomitable resolve to make myself shine while being ordinary.

I thought to myself, "It is alright to be ordinary. I will try to accumulate outstanding results while living as an ordinary person. No, I do not even need to attain great achievements; small achievements are fine. I just want to lead the kind of life I can be proud of—the kind of life that others will be glad that I lived—and steadily build up positive results." When I realized this and put it into practice, the devils left me. They could no longer appear before me.

I assume that there are many of you who are interested in spiritual matters. Some of you may actually possess some spiritual abilities. If so, you must not simply seek to be exceptional. When you do, know that you are standing on the edge of a cliff. You need to be aware that in your desire to be exceptional there is a desire for fame, which is what devils prey on.

When you find such a mistake in your thoughts, try to live in ordinariness. Seek the light in ordinariness. Try to make a fresh start from the ordinary once again. I want you to think about whether you can call yourself a truly good and admirable person, and whether there was any meaning to you being born in this life, even if your spiritual abilities were to be removed. When you can answer "yes" to these questions, you have truly triumphed over the devils, and even more importantly, you have conquered the devil within.

5

Death, Then Life

In my confrontations with the devils, I experienced very tough soul training day after day for five to six years. I made efforts to emit brilliant light in my ordinariness and build up positive results. As I approached the age of 30, however, something extraordinary began to emerge from my accumulation of ordinary achievements.

Around that time, my father, Saburo Yoshikawa, succeeded in compiling the spiritual messages I had received into book form and getting them published. We began to put out books continuously, about once every two months, such as *The Spiritual Messages from Saint Nichiren*, *The Spiritual Messages from Kukai*, and *The Spiritual Messages from Christ*.

Those days were truly difficult for me. I was approaching the age that would allow me to join the ranks of middle management, and the path to career advancement was open before me. I still retained much desire to develop my strengths further in the business world and fulfill my potential. At the same time, I also felt I could not continue in that manner—I knew I had to somehow carry out the special mission I had been given. Those two feelings were in conflict in my mind.

Part of the problem was probably the fear of stepping out into an unknown world. Even though I was receiving spiritual revelations from high spirits, I agonized over how to spread this Truth to the world, what kind of mission to start based on the Truth, and how I could open up this path at the tender age of almost 30.

It was around this time that I reached a turning point, as described in *The Laws of the Sun*. I think it was just before my 30th birthday. All the spirits that I had been communicating with started to send me the same message: "Now is the time to rise." And finally, I made up my mind to abandon my work at the company and stand up on my own to live for the Truth.

Until then, I had intended to continue earning a livelihood through some other work while simultaneously carrying out my activities for the Truth, balancing the two activities. However, I finally made up my mind and told myself, "I do not need income. I do not want anything. I need nothing. I am just going to do what I want to do. I will die for the Truth, and I will not be afraid of losing my life. If I die within a year, so be it."

When I left the company, I think I had just enough in my savings to support myself for one year. I thought to myself, "It would be OK if I died after a year. I will do all that I can. I will do what I want to do without worrying about the future. At any rate, I want to do this. I can't stand it anymore. I want to enter the path of the Truth. I want to go straight ahead on the path to the Truth. I don't care about my past career. I don't care about my reputation. Even if people think that I am an evil man or that I have gone mad, I don't care at all about what they think of me. People may ridicule me for being a founder of a religious group or call me crazy, but I won't care what they say. I will completely abandon everything, and 'die' at this very moment."

That moment marked the birth of Ryuho Okawa. At that time, I had a different name, which had been officially registered at my birth, but I decided to abandon my original name and live under my religious name, Ryuho Okawa. I underwent my first "death" at the age of 24, and the second "death" at the age of 30. The person who had been working hard at a trading company completely "died." I thus cast off my entire past.

At the same time, I also gave up all my previous relationships. I broke off my relationships with my old friends, my colleagues, my superiors, and my subordinates. I cut off my old life entirely. I also gave up my hopes for the future. I rose up with the determination to throw away everything and start empty-handed to establish Happy Science. This was my second death.

By abandoning myself, I was reborn. The first few months were quite hard; I had no income and no prospects. All I had were the words of the high spirits and my own will. I lived with these as my only crutch in life. However, discarding my old self in this way served as the key to great development. Because of my awareness of having died twice, I was no longer afraid of anything that could happen.

There is nothing to be afraid of for those who can abandon everything at any given time. Even as I am spreading the Truth now, I have nothing to fear because I am ready to abandon everything and start over again empty-handed at any point; I am always prepared to start again with nothing at hand. This state of mind was, in fact, the powerful first step to becoming an Enlightened One—an Awakened One.

There have always been such moments of awakening, in all time periods. Shakyamuni Buddha once experienced this great moment. The details and the environment may differ, but the state of mind is always the same: the determination to live for the sake of the true world and the will to rise up in the world with the understanding of one's true nature and awareness of spiritual views of life. It is my sincere hope that many people will also have this kind of experience.

6

To the Extraordinary Heights of Love

Having experienced the second death and been reborn, I have given everything to fulfill my mission. I am now filled with the feeling that "It no longer matters when Ryuho Okawa dies. If I can live for many people—for those living today and those of future generations— I would be happy. If possible, I want to leave behind something that will last for 2,000 or 3,000 years in the future. I want to create something that will give nourishment to the souls of a great number of people. I want to become like the water of an oasis in the desert, which never runs dry no matter how much is drawn out. I want to become like such a spring. I want to be the source of the Law."

My activities will continue on; they will most probably expand both in quality and quantity. As our movement becomes more and more active, there may be times when we are misunderstood or mocked. There is already a certain group of people who claim that our work is carried out for the sake of personal glory or for moneymaking, but such criticisms are insignificant and trivial. These criticisms may show that these people always harbor such kinds of negative thoughts, but as someone who has already died twice, I am not at all affected by these words.

I have an indomitable fighting spirit which can only be possessed by those who have abandoned themselves. People who have never experienced this sort of spiritual death can never understand this state. There is a truth that can only be understood by those who have experienced spiritual death, who have abandoned their pride, their future, and everything that belonged to them.

Since I have started out from the ordinary and lived an ordinary life, I do not mind if I am buried in ordinariness. I am satisfied as long as what I leave behind remains as an exceptional achievement. I want to leave such achievements as an extraordinary gift for the people of future generations. Personal glory means nothing to me, and worldly success does not mean anything to me either. I will simply do what needs to be done and do what my heart tells me.

I am plowing the land. On seeing how I am tilling the land, various people may comment that my hand movements are awkward or my back is not balanced, and say a variety of things. However, my mission will not be completed until I have tilled every bit of this ground.

From now on, I will continuously bring the Truth to the world. As long as I am alive, as long as I live, as long as I have life on Earth, and as long as there are fellow believers who encourage and support me, I would like to keep on leading an ordinary life, wishing that what is left behind will soar to the extraordinary heights of love. I believe that someday, when my life on Earth comes to a close, the accumulation of such ordinariness will ascend to heaven and shed the sublime light of love. With this pure intention, I began this work and would like to complete it.

Afterword to the Original Edition

I look upon the publication of this book as my first milestone. I believe that explaining the basic philosophical process I had before establishing Happy Science and my own standpoint will serve to further expand my publishing work in the future.

Even though this book is written in a literary and lyrical fashion, it is also a work of philosophy and enlightenment. I am sure it will help accelerate the spiritual progress of my readers.

Ryuho Okawa
Master and CEO of Happy Science Group
July 1988

Afterword to the New Edition

As I reread this book, which was originally written 14 years ago, various emotions from the past reemerged. Even though my ideas were not yet fully developed, this book reveals the origins of my thoughts, so in this sense, it is already considered a "classic" among Happy Science believers. I thought it would be wasteful for it to remain out of print.

To tell the truth, my eldest daughter, who is entering the sixth grade this year, was carefully reading a copy of the book over and over again, highlighting important passages with markers, during breaks in her studies for the junior high entrance examination. On seeing her, I realized that this book is one of the few introductory works that would help young readers understand the philosophy of Ryuho Okawa. While Chapters Three and Five are a little difficult, Chapters One, Two, Four, and Six contain material that can be helpful to young people as well.

Moreover, after my eldest daughter started to read this book and *The Laws of the Sun* thoroughly, her reading and writing skills improved significantly to the point where she started to frequently receive full marks on tests, not only in school but also at cram school. I was surprised by this change, and thought that if there were such unexpected benefits, I must publish more introductory books like this for the sake of the children of Happy Science believers.

In my family, we instruct our children, including our little one who is not yet of primary school age, to study and read *The Rebirth of Buddha*[*] aloud. These days, I strongly feel I should write more books that even children can understand.

---

[*] TF: *The Rebirth of Buddha* (Tokyo: Happy Science, 2009) is available in English at Happy Science locations (see Contact Information p.189).

I sincerely hope that the attitude of starting from the ordinary, the spirit of being independent, and the experience of enlightenment described in this book will become nourishment for the souls of young people.

Ryuho Okawa
Master and CEO of Happy Science Group
July 2002

TN: The two afterwords were given for Part One, "El Cantare in Youth."

PART TWO

The Victory of Faith

Lecture given on July 15, 1991
at Tokyo Dome, Japan

1

The Declaration of El Cantare

All of you, my disciples,
I am sincerely grateful to you
For coming to celebrate my 35th birthday today.

Of all that you can experience on Earth,
The miracle called faith has the greatest power.
Faith is the power
That makes all the impossible possible.
It eliminates all difficulties,
Makes all suffering disappear,
And opens the direct road to God.

Now, read my book *The Eternal Buddha**
That has already been given to you.
The Will I put in the words in the book—
Do you think
These words came from a human being?
Do you think
They are the thoughts of a human?

---

* TF: *The Eternal Buddha* (Tokyo: Happy Science, 2009) is available in English at Happy Science locations (see Contact Information p.189).

You must not be misled
By the physical appearance
Of a human called Ryuho Okawa.
The one who stands before you
Is Ryuho Okawa,
Yet not Ryuho Okawa.
The one who stands before you
And teaches the eternal Truth
Is El Cantare.

I am the one
Who holds the highest authority on this Earth.
I am the one
Who has full authority regarding this Earth
From its beginning to its end
Because I am not a human being,
But the Law itself.

2

The Eternal Buddha

You must not be deluded
By your physical eyes.
God, or the Eternal Buddha
That represents and expresses God,
Is not a human being.
It is the Law.
It is the Teaching.
It is the Rule.
It is the Teaching that governs this great universe.

This universe was not created by chance.
There is no coincidence in the heavens above.
There is no coincidence on the earth below.
Everything,
Even the falling of a single leaf,
Comes under God's Law.

How great God is—
Since the far-distant past,
Long before this great universe was created,
God existed as Will.
This Will embraced all,

Loved all,

Nurtured all,

And commanded,

"All my creations, be great.

Be great as I am."

This is how each and every one of your souls was created.

Just because your souls reside in small physical bodies

Of less than two meters in size,

You must not think of yourselves as petty.

You must not think of yourselves as insignificant.

What I have engraved deep within your souls

Are imperishable wisdom

And immortal power.

Find that wisdom and that power within you.

At that time,

You will know that each and every one of you is endowed

With the same light as the Eternal Buddha—

Exactly the same light as God.

To have faith does not mean

To worship an unseen Being

That exists in a far-off place.

Within each and every one of you

Is the great existence of God.

3

The Greatest Happiness:

The Freedom of the Soul

Ah, despite this,
What kind of life have you been living
In the decades since you were born into this world?
Has it been the right way to live
As a child of God?
Can you swear to yourself
That your life of several decades has truly not been shameful
As someone who carries God's light within?

Even so,
I do not blame you
For being immature.
Being immature also means
You have infinite potential for progress.
However,
If this potential for progress is left unfulfilled,
Who is to blame?
Who bears the sin for it?
No one but each one of you
Can bear that sin.

In essence, everyone has the same power as God.
This means
Each one of you bears complete responsibility
For your entire life.
Taking full responsibility means that
It was each one of you who made decisions
When you yourself were required to make choices
In the course of your life.
This is the freedom of the soul.
This freedom of the soul is
The greatest happiness that is inside you.

Some of you may deny the existence of God
Using words or logic,
And ask,
"If God is absolute perfection
And if we are children of God,
Why do humans commit evil?
Why do sadness and suffering exist in life?"
However, such questions do not serve or prove
As your excuse for living an imperfect life.
It is precisely because we are given complete freedom
That we can make our own choice
From all the possible options.

Those who have been through sadness and found delight
Have attained the greatest happiness.
There is no room for unhappiness to creep up
To those who knew suffering

And yet were able to overcome it to attain glory.
Yes, you must know what a blessing it is
To have freedom in the truest sense—
Freedom of being the master of your own soul.

Then you shall realize
That God's loving hand
Holds even the depths of hell,
Which you may loathe.
God sustains even the world of hell,
Where several billion souls are suffering.
God holds it and embraces it.
You must know this fact.
You must never forget that
There is a Being embracing hell,
Dreaming of the day
When the suffering turns into the greatest happiness.

4

Happy Science: The Light to Save Earth

You are not alone or without support.
This is not only about this world.
There are only about five billion people living on Earth,*
But in the heavenly world, far beyond this world,
There are more than 50 billion spirits
Living in the Earth's sphere.
What is more,
Myriads of solar systems exist outside our own.
In those solar systems, too,
Humanlike beings undergo spiritual discipline every day
To attain happiness,
Just like all of you.

Then,
Your views of life must not be built
On what you have experienced
In the past several decades of your life.
What is the mission
Of the Earth's spirit group of over 50 billion?

---

* TF: The world population at the time of the lecture.

What is our mission in this great universe?
You must also take these things into consideration.

We are the light of hope in this galaxy.
While being the light of hope,
We are also being watched with great concern
By the beings of other planets in the galaxy.
They are concerned:
"In which direction is Earth heading?"

I have already made many predictions.
You may have found
Many of them to be colored by terrifying realities.
However, they are just warnings—
Warnings to humanity
And warnings to you all.
In the coming decade,
The last 10 years of this century,
Countless natural disasters, wars,
And the deaths of many are expected to occur.

But I dare say that
They are just plans.
They are mere prospects.
I am just saying that
These events will happen if nothing changes.
This is because
Light and darkness are relative to each other on Earth.
If light grows stronger,

Darkness draws back,
And if darkness gets stronger,
Light appears to pull back for some time.
The solution to the equation
Made up of these two simple variables
Will be determined in the next 10 years.

You must understand deeply
Why we, Happy Science, rose to spread the Truth
With all our might.
Do you think it is out of our mere self-interest?
Do you think it is a movement of a single religious sect?
It is by no means out of a selfish desire
To benefit an individual called Ryuho Okawa.
Our movement of Truth *is* the Light to save Earth.

Quite a few candles have now been lit in Japan.
You are the flames of these candles
That have been lit in such a short time.
How encouraging these lights look.

However, however, however, however,
Leave your physical body
And look at Earth from the distant universe.
Imagine how Earth would look.
The blue Earth is about to sink into darkness.
Its surface is being clouded and covered by dark thoughts,
Starting to block the light of God.
And a dark age is about to begin.

Imagine how unreliable and feeble
The flames of these candles are
When viewed from the distant sky.
They just barely seem to flicker
In this small, small country called Japan.

5

Pledge to God

Whether or not you can prevent
The terrifying revelations of Nostradamus and other prophets
From happening in the future
Depends on your activities.
It may not be possible to change them all.
We have already reached a point
Where we cannot change everything.
Even so,
There is still a chance to alter
The way these fearful prophecies are realized.
Our future will be determined
By how much light, energy, and power
This movement of Truth will bear.

So, I dare say unto you.
Now is the time to make a pledge to God
With a pure heart.

It is the Master who teaches the Law,
And it is the disciples who spread it.
My disciples, make up your mind.

In this lifetime,
You are not allowed to let your life end
Without accomplishing your mission.
Otherwise,
You would be breaking your pledge to God.

Yet, my wish is not limited to things so small.
We are not only responsible
For the people who are alive.
We must also save the billions of lost souls
Who lived before us and are now in hell,
Suffering the infernal fires.
It is Happy Science's fighters of Light
Who must now open the gates of hell,
Bring forgiveness to their sins,
And guide them to the world of Light.
Your work is the most sacred
And the most precious
Throughout all the centuries on Earth,
The past, present, and future.

6

The Ideal of Creating Buddha Land

Believe. Believe. Believe.
Believe in me.
Believe in the Eternal Buddha.
Believe that the Eternal Buddha has appeared
And is teaching the eternal Truth in front of you.
Once you believe,
You will only see victory prevail before you.

Listen.
Before I leave this world,
Spread the Truth not only in Japan
But to the entire world
And to all five billion or so people.
Spread the eternal Truth,
The eternal Law,
The everlasting Law
That flows from the Eternal Buddha.

Listen.
Every one of your lives is infinitely precious.
Your life is precious

Because it contains within
Limited time in this world.
Your lives have been imbued with time.
Even if a soul lives eternally
Through the past, present, and future,
There is no moment
More precious than the present to be born.

Listen.
I was born 2,600 years ago
As Shakyamuni Buddha of India.
I was born 4,300 years ago
As Hermes of Greece.
But the soul
Now appearing before you as Ryuho Okawa
Is El Cantare—
The core consciousness of the soul of the Buddha.
You are witnesses to such a moment.

This movement of Truth must not remain small.
Just filling Tokyo Dome with light is not enough.

To the 50,000 disciples who have gathered here.
To the thousands or tens of thousands
Of tathagatas and bodhisattvas
Who have come today.
To the beings of Light in heaven.
Give us power.

Give power to our sacred wish.
Give us infinite Light.
Allow us to realize our ideal of creating Buddha Land.

7

The Victory of Faith

All of you, my disciples,
You must not perceive my words
Only as vibrations upon your ears.
That would be very sad, indeed.
Embrace the spiritual power of my words
With your soul.
After you leave this world,
You will no longer have any chance
Of listening directly to my teachings in the heavenly world.
So now, in this place,
Engrave in your souls these words I speak
As golden words.
Inscribe them.
Engrave this day: July 15, 1991
In your souls.
You must never forget this day,
For this is a milestone in our journey
To save all humankind.

Stand up with me.
Gather under my White Hand.
Follow behind me,

And let us begin to walk the march of Light.
The world is entrusted upon us.
If we fail to bring salvation to the entire world
It will solely be because of our own negligence.

Everything is possible.
In the name of faith,
You will only see victory.
Know this truth.
Faith will give you the greatest victory.

Remember the pledge you have made to the angels of Light
Here in this dome today.
Never forget that
You have exchanged vows with the angels of Light
In your souls today.
As long as I live,
I shall spread the Truth.
I ask you to follow suit.

The Eternal Buddha is here.
And His disciples are here.
Let us work together to fulfill our mission.

ABOUT THE AUTHOR

RYUHO OKAWA was born on July 7th 1956, in Tokushima, Japan. After graduating from the University of Tokyo with a law degree, he joined a Tokyo-based trading house. While working at its New York headquarters, he studied international finance at the Graduate Center of the City University of New York. In 1981, he attained Great Enlightenment and became aware that he is El Cantare with a mission to bring salvation to all of humankind. In 1986, he established Happy Science. It now has members in over 100 countries across the world, with more than 700 local branches and temples as well as 10,000 missionary houses around the world. The total number of lectures has exceeded 3,150 (of which more than 150 are in English) and over 2,700 books (of which more than 550 are Spiritual Interview Series) have been published, many of which are translated into 31 languages. Many of the books, including *The Laws of the Sun* have become best sellers or million sellers. To date, Happy Science has produced 20 movies. The original story and original concept were given by the Executive Producer Ryuho Okawa. Recent movie titles are *The Real Exorcist* (live-action, May 2020), *Living in the Age of Miracles* (documentary, Aug. 2020), and *Twiceborn* (live-action, scheduled to be released in Oct. 2020). He has also composed the lyrics and music of over 100 songs, such as theme songs and featured songs of movies. Moreover, he is the Founder of Happy Science University and Happy Science Academy (Junior and Senior High School), Founder and President of the Happiness Realization Party, Founder and Honorary Headmaster of Happy Science Institute of Government and Management, Founder of IRH Press Co., Ltd., and the Chairperson of New Star Production Co., Ltd. and ARI Production Co., Ltd.

WHAT IS EL CANTARE?

El Cantare means "the Light of the Earth," and is the Supreme God of the Earth who has been guiding humankind since the beginning of Genesis. He is whom Jesus called Father and Muhammad called Allah. Different parts of El Cantare's core consciousness have descended to Earth in the past, once as Alpha and another as Elohim. His branch spirits, such as Shakyamuni Buddha and Hermes, have descended to Earth many times and helped to flourish many civilizations. To unite various religions and to integrate various fields of study in order to build a new civilization on Earth, a part of the core consciousness has descended to Earth as Master Ryuho Okawa.

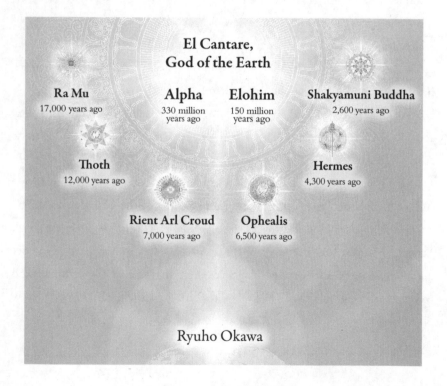

**El Cantare,
God of the Earth**

Ra Mu
17,000 years ago

Alpha
330 million
years ago

Elohim
150 million
years ago

Shakyamuni Buddha
2,600 years ago

Thoth
12,000 years ago

Hermes
4,300 years ago

Rient Arl Croud
7,000 years ago

Ophealis
6,500 years ago

Ryuho Okawa

Alpha is a part of the core consciousness of El Cantare who descended to Earth around 330 million years ago. Alpha preached Earth's Truths to harmonize and unify Earth-born humans and space people who came from other planets.

Elohim is a part of El Cantare's core consciousness who descended to Earth around 150 million years ago. He gave wisdom, mainly on the differences of light and darkness, good and evil.

Shakyamuni Buddha was born as a prince into the Shakya Clan in India around 2,600 years ago. When he was 29 years old, he renounced the world and sought enlightenment. He later attained Great Enlightenment and founded Buddhism.

Hermes is one of the 12 Olympian gods in Greek mythology, but the spiritual Truth is that he taught the teachings of love and progress around 4,300 years ago that became the origin of the current Western civilization. He is a hero that truly existed.

Ophealis was born in Greece around 6,500 years ago and was the leader who took an expedition to as far as Egypt. He is the God of miracles, prosperity, and arts, and is known as Osiris in the Egyptian mythology.

Rient Arl Croud was born as a king of the ancient Incan Empire around 7,000 years ago and taught about the mysteries of the mind. In the heavenly world, he is responsible for the interactions that take place between various planets.

Thoth was an almighty leader who built the golden age of the Atlantic civilization around 12,000 years ago. In the Egyptian mythology, he is known as god Thoth.

Ra Mu was a leader who built the golden age of the civilization of Mu around 17,000 years ago. As a religious leader and a politician, he ruled by uniting religion and politics.

WHAT IS A SPIRITUAL MESSAGE?

We are all spiritual beings living on this earth. The following is the mechanism behind Master Ryuho Okawa's spiritual messages.

1 You are a spirit

People are born into this world to gain wisdom through various experiences and return to the other world when their lives end. We are all spirits and repeat this cycle in order to refine our souls.

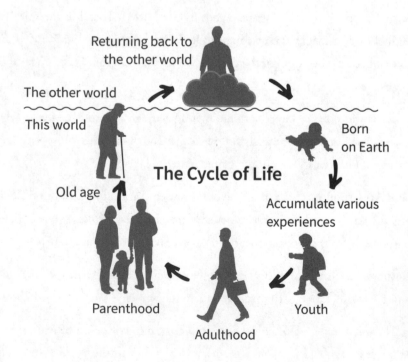

Returning back to the other world

The other world

This world

Born on Earth

Old age

The Cycle of Life

Accumulate various experiences

Parenthood

Adulthood

Youth

2 You have a guardian spirit

Guardian spirits are those who protect the people who are living on this earth. Each of us has a guardian spirit that watches over us and guides us from the other world. They were us in our past life, and are identical in how we think.

3 How spiritual messages work

Master Ryuho Okawa, through his enlightenment, is capable of summoning any spirit from anywhere in the world, including the spirit world.

Master Okawa's way of receiving spiritual messages is fundamentally different from that of other psychic mediums who undergo trances and are thereby completely taken over by the spirits they are channeling.

Master Okawa's attainment of a high level of enlightenment enables him to retain full control of his consciousness and body throughout the duration of the spiritual message. To allow the spirits to express their own thoughts and personalities freely, however, Master Okawa usually softens the dominancy of his consciousness. This way, he is able to keep his own philosophies out of the way and ensure that the spiritual messages are pure expressions of the spirits he is channeling.

Since guardian spirits think at the same subconscious level as the person living on earth, Master Okawa can summon the spirit and find out what the person on earth is actually thinking. If the person has already returned to the other world, the spirit can give messages to the people living on earth through Master Okawa.

Since 2009, more than 1,100 sessions of spiritual messages have been openly recorded by Master Okawa, and the majority of these have been published. Spiritual messages from the guardian spirits of people living today such as Donald Trump, Japanese Prime Minister Shinzo Abe and Chinese President Xi Jinping, as well as spiritual messages sent from the spirit world by Jesus Christ, Muhammad, Thomas Edison, Mother Teresa, Steve Jobs and Nelson Mandela are just a tiny pack of spiritual messages that were published so far.

Domestically, in Japan, these spiritual messages are being read by a wide range of politicians and mass media, and the high-level contents of these books are delivering an impact even more on politics, news and public opinion. In recent years, there have been spiritual messages recorded in

English, and English translations are being done on the spiritual messages given in Japanese. These have been published overseas, one after another, and have started to shake the world.

1 The guardian spirit /
spirit in the other world...

2 Goes inside Master Okawa
in this world

3 Master Okawa speaks
the words of the guardian spirit /
spirit

*For more about spiritual messages and a complete list of books in the Spiritual Interview Series, visit **okawabooks.com***

ABOUT HAPPY SCIENCE

Happy Science is a global movement that empowers individuals to find purpose and spiritual happiness and to share that happiness with their families, societies, and the world. With more than 12 million members around the world, Happy Science aims to increase awareness of spiritual truths and expand our capacity for love, compassion, and joy so that together we can create the kind of world we all wish to live in.

Activities at Happy Science are based on the principles of happiness (love, wisdom, self-reflection, and progress). These principles embrace worldwide philosophies and beliefs, transcending boundaries of culture and religions.

Love teaches us to give ourselves freely without expecting anything in return; it encompasses giving, nurturing, and forgiving.

Wisdom leads us to the insights of spiritual truths, and opens us to the true meaning of life and the will of God (the universe, the highest power, Buddha).

Self-Reflection brings a mindful, nonjudgmental lens to our thoughts and actions to help us find our truest selves—the essence of our souls—and deepen our connection to the highest power. It helps us attain a clean and peaceful mind and leads us to the right life path.

Progress emphasizes the positive, dynamic aspects of our spiritual growth—actions we can take to manifest and spread happiness around the world. It's a path that not only expands our soul growth, but also furthers the collective potential of the world we live in.

PROGRAMS AND EVENTS

The doors of Happy Science are open to all. We offer a variety of programs and events, including self-exploration and self-growth programs, spiritual seminars, meditation and contemplation sessions, study groups, and book events.

Our programs are designed to:
* Deepen your understanding of your purpose and meaning in life
* Improve your relationships and increase your capacity to love unconditionally
* Attain peace of mind, decrease anxiety and stress, and feel positive
* Gain deeper insights and a broader perspective on the world
* Learn how to overcome life's challenges
  ... and much more.

*For more information, visit **happy-science.org**.*

INTERNATIONAL SEMINARS

Each year, friends from all over the world join our international seminars, held at our faith centers in Japan. Different programs are offered each year and cover a wide variety of topics, including improving relationships, practicing the Eightfold Path to enlightenment, and loving yourself, to name just a few.

HAPPY SCIENCE MONTHLY

Happy Science regularly publishes various magazines for readers around the world. The Happy Science Monthly, which now spans over 300 issues, contains Master Okawa's latest lectures, words of wisdom, stories of remarkable life-changing experiences, world news, and much more to guide members and their friends to a happier life. This is available in many other languages, including Portuguese, Spanish, French, German, Chinese, and Korean. Happy Science Basics, on the other hand, is a 'theme-based' booklet made in an easy-to-read style for those new to Happy Science, which is also ideal to give to friends and family. You can pick up the latest issues from Happy Science, subscribe to have them delivered (see our contacts page) or view them online.*

* Online editions of the *Happy Science Monthly* and *Happy Science Basics* can be viewed at:
info.happy-science.org/category/magazines/

CONTACT INFORMATION

Happy Science is a worldwide organization with faith centers around the globe. For a comprehensive list of centers, visit the worldwide directory at *happy-science.org*. The following are some of the many Happy Science locations:

UNITED STATES AND CANADA

New York
79 Franklin St., New York, NY 10013
Phone: 212-343-7972
Fax: 212-343-7973
Email: ny@happy-science.org
Website: happyscience-na.org

New Jersey
725 River Rd, #102B, Edgewater, NJ 07020
Phone: 201-313-0127
Fax: 201-313-0120
Email: nj@happy-science.org
Website: happyscience-na.org

Florida
5208 8th St., St. Zephyrhills, FL 33542
Phone: 813-715-0000
Fax: 813-715-0010
Email: florida@happy-science.org
Website: happyscience-na.org

Atlanta
1874 Piedmont Ave., NE Suite 360-C
Atlanta, GA 30324
Phone: 404-892-7770
Email: atlanta@happy-science.org
Website: happyscience-na.org

San Francisco
525 Clinton St.
Redwood City, CA 94062
Phone & Fax: 650-363-2777
Email: sf@happy-science.org
Website: happyscience-na.org

Los Angeles
1590 E. Del Mar Blvd., Pasadena, CA 91106
Phone: 626-395-7775
Fax: 626-395-7776
Email: la@happy-science.org
Website: happyscience-na.org

Orange County
10231 Slater Ave., #204
Fountain Valley, CA 92708
Phone: 714-745-1140
Email: oc@happy-science.org
Website: happyscience-na.org

San Diego
7841 Balboa Ave., Suite #202
San Diego, CA 92111
Phone: 626-395-7775
Fax: 626-395-7776
E-mail: sandiego@happy-science.org
Website: happyscience-na.org

Hawaii

Phone: 808-591-9772
Fax: 808-591-9776
Email: hi@happy-science.org
Website: happyscience-na.org

Kauai

3343 Kanakolu Street, Suite 5
Lihue, HI 96766, U.S.A.
Phone: 808-822-7007
Fax: 808-822-6007
Email: kauai-hi@happy-science.org
Website: kauai.happyscience-na.org

Toronto

845 The Queensway
Etobicoke ON M8Z 1N6 Canada
Phone: 1-416-901-3747
Email: toronto@happy-science.org
Website: happy-science.ca

Vancouver

#201-2607 East 49th Avenue
Vancouver, BC, V5S 1J9, Canada
Phone: 1-604-437-7735
Fax: 1-604-437-7764
Email: vancouver@happy-science.org
Website: happy-science.ca

INTERNATIONAL

Tokyo

1-6-7 Togoshi, Shinagawa
Tokyo, 142-0041 Japan
Phone: 81-3-6384-5770
Fax: 81-3-6384-5776
Email: tokyo@happy-science.org
Website: happy-science.org

London

3 Margaret St.
London,W1W 8RE United Kingdom
Phone: 44-20-7323-9255
Fax: 44-20-7323-9344
Email: eu@happy-science.org
Website: happyscience-uk.org

Sydney

516 Pacific Hwy, Lane Cove North,
NSW 2066, Australia
Phone: 61-2-9411-2877
Fax: 61-2-9411-2822
Email: sydney@happy-science.org

Seoul

74, Sadang-ro 27-gil,
Dongjak-gu, Seoul, Korea
Phone: 82-2-3478-8777
Fax: 82-2-3478-9777
Email: korea@happy-science.org
Website: happyscience-korea.org

Brazil Headquarters

Rua. Domingos de Morais 1154,
Vila Mariana, Sao Paulo SP
CEP 04009-002, Brazil
Phone: 55-11-5088-3800
Fax: 55-11-5088-3806
Email: sp@happy-science.org
Website: happyscience.com.br

Jundiai

Rua Congo, 447, Jd. Bonfiglioli
Jundiai-CEP, 13207-340
Phone: 55-11-4587-5952
Email: jundiai@happy-science.org

Taipei

No. 89, Lane 155, Dunhua N. Road
Songshan District, Taipei City 105, Taiwan
Phone: 886-2-2719-9377
Fax: 886-2-2719-5570
Email: taiwan@happy-science.org
Website: happyscience-tw.org

Malaysia

No 22A, Block 2, Jalil Link Jalan Jalil Jaya 2, Bukit
Jalil 57000, Kuala Lumpur, Malaysia
Phone: 60-3-8998-7877
Fax: 60-3-8998-7977
Email: malaysia@happy-science.org
Website: happyscience.org.my

Nepal

Kathmandu Metropolitan City Ward
No. 15,
Ring Road, Kimdol,
Sitapaila Kathmandu, Nepal
Phone: 97-714-272931
Email: nepal@happy-science.org

Uganda

Plot 877 Rubaga Road, Kampala
P.O. Box 34130, Kampala, Uganda
Phone: 256-79-4682-121
Email: uganda@happy-science.org
Website: happyscience-uganda.org

Thailand

19 Soi Sukhumvit 60/1,
Bang Chak, Phra Khanong,
Bangkok, 10260 Thailand
Phone: 66-2-007-1419
Email: bangkok@happy-science.org
Website: happyscience-thai.org

Indonesia

Darmawangsa
Square Lt. 2 No. 225
Jl. Darmawangsa VI & IX
Indonesia
Phone: 021-7278-0756
Email: indonesia@happy-science.org

Philippines Taytay

LGL Bldg, 2nd Floor,
Kadalagaham cor,
Rizal Ave. Taytay,
Rizal, Philippines
Phone: 63-2-5710686
Email: philippines@happy-science.org

SOCIAL CONTRIBUTIONS

Happy Science tackles social issues such as suicide and bullying, and launches heartfelt, precise and prompt rescue operations after a major disaster.

◆ The HS Nelson Mandela Fund

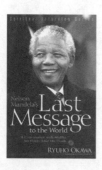

The Happy Science Group provides disaster relief and educational aid overseas via this Fund. We established it following the publication of *Nelson Mandela's Last Message to the World*, a spiritual message from the late Nelson Mandela, in 2013. The fund actively provides both material and spiritual aid to people overseas—support for victims of racial discrimination, poverty, political oppression, natural disasters, and more.

Examples of how the fund has been used:

Provided tents in rural Nepal

Supplied food and water immediately after the Nepal earthquake

Donated a container library to South African primary school, in collaboration with Nelson Mandela Foundation

◆ **We extend a helping hand around the world to aid in post-disaster reconstruction and education.**

NEPAL: From 2015 to 2020 after the Nepal Earthquake, we promptly changed our local temple into a temporary evacuation center and utilized our global network to send water, food and tents. We still keep supporting the rebuilding of schools.

SRI LANKA: Provided aid in constructing school buildings damaged by the tsunami. Further, with the help of the Sri Lankan prime minister, 100 bookshelves were donated to Buddhist temples.

INDIA: Ongoing aid since 2006—uniforms, school meals, etc. for schools in Bodh Gaya, a sacred ground for Buddhism. Medical aid in Kolkata, in collaboration with local hospitals.

CHINA: Donated money and tents to the Szechuan Earthquake disaster zone. Books were also donated to elementary schools in Gansu Province, near the disaster zone.

UGANDA: Donated educational materials and mosquito nets to protect children from Malaria. Donated a school building and prayer hall to a private secondary school, as well as offering a scholarship to a university student who had graduated from the school.

GHANA: Provided medical supplies as a preventive measure against Ebola.

SOUTH AFRICA: Collaborated with the Nelson Mandela Foundation in South Africa to donate a container library and books to an elementary school.

IRAN: Donated to the earthquake-stricken area in northeastern Iran in October 2012, and donated 15,000 masks as medical aid in May 2020 via the Iranian Embassy.

ABOUT HAPPINESS REALIZATION PARTY

The Happiness Realization Party (HRP) was founded in May 2009 by Master Ryuho Okawa as part of the Happy Science Group to offer concrete and proactive solutions to the current issues such as military threats from North Korea and China and the long-term economic recession. HRP aims to implement drastic reforms of the Japanese government, thereby bringing peace and prosperity to Japan. To accomplish this, HRP proposes two key policies:

1) Strengthening the national security and the Japan-U.S. alliance which plays a vital role in the stability of Asia.

2) Improving the Japanese economy by implementing drastic tax cuts, taking monetary easing measures and creating new major industries.

HRP advocates that Japan should offer a model of a religious nation that allows diverse values and beliefs to coexist, and that contributes to global peace.

*For more information, visit **en.hr-party.jp***

HAPPY SCIENCE ACADEMY
JUNIOR AND SENIOR HIGH SCHOOL

Happy Science Academy Junior and Senior High School is a boarding school founded with the goal of educating the future leaders of the world who can have a big vision, persevere, and take on new challenges.

Currently, there are two campuses in Japan; the Nasu Main Campus in Tochigi Prefecture, founded in 2010, and the Kansai Campus in Shiga Prefecture, founded in 2013.

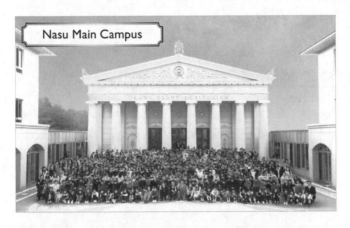

Nasu Main Campus

Kansai Campus

HAPPY SCIENCE UNIVERSITY

THE FOUNDING SPIRIT AND THE GOAL OF EDUCATION

Based on the founding philosophy of the university, "Exploration of happiness and the creation of a new civilization," education, research and studies will be provided to help students acquire deep understanding grounded in religious belief and advanced expertise with the objectives of producing "great talents of virtue" who can contribute in a broad-ranging way to serve Japan and the international society.

FACULTIES

Faculty of Human Happiness

Students in this faculty will pursue liberal arts from various perspectives with a multidisciplinary approach, explore and envision an ideal state of human beings and society.

Faculty of Successful Management

This faculty aims to realize successful management that helps organizations to create value and wealth for society and to contribute to the happiness and the development of management and employees as well as society as a whole.

Faculty of Future Creation

Students in this faculty study subjects such as political science, journalism, performing arts and artistic expression, and explore and present new political and cultural models based on truth, goodness and beauty.

Faculty of Future Industry

This faculty aims to nurture engineers who can resolve various issues facing modern civilization from a technological standpoint and contribute to the creation of new industries of the future.

ABOUT HAPPY SCIENCE MOVIES

TWICEBORN

Coming to Theaters Fall 2020

STORY Satoru Ichijo receives a message from the spiritual world and realizes his mission is to lead humankind to happiness. He became a successful businessman while publishing spiritual messages secretly, but the devil's temptation shakes his mind and...

Documentary

LIVING IN THE AGE OF MIRACLES

An inspirational documentary about two Japanese actors meeting people who experienced miracles in their lives. Through their quest, they find the key to working miracles and learn what "living in the age of miracles" truly means.

WINNER
AWARD OF MERIT
SPECIAL MENTION
IMPACT DOCS AWARDS

GOLD AWARD
Documentary Feature
International
Independent Film Awards
Spring 2020

GOLD AWARD
Concept
International
Independent Film Awards
Spring 2020

Documentary

LIFE IS BEAUTIFUL

Six people seeking their purposes of life

BRONZE REMI AWARD
53rd WORLDFEST HOUSTON
INTERNATIONAL FILM
FESTIVAL 2020

WINNER
BEST
EDITING OF A
DOCUMENTARY
NICE
2020

IMMORTAL HERO

`On VOD NOW`

Based on the true story of a man whose near death experience inspires him
to choose life... and change the lives of millions.

40 Awards from 9 Countries!

SPAIN
BARCELONA INTERNATIONAL
FILM FESTIVAL 2019
[THE CASTELL AWARDS]

SPAIN
MADRID INTERNATIONAL
FILM FESTIVAL 2019
[BEST DIRECTOR OF A FOREIGN
LANGUAGE FEATURE FILM]

ITALY
FLORENCE FILM AWARDS JUL 2019
[HONORABLE MENTION:
FEATURE FILM]

USA
INDIE VISIONS FILM FESTIVAL
JUL 2019 [WINNER (NARRATIVE
FEATURE FILM)]

ITALY
FLORENCE FILM AWARDS JUL 2019
[BEST ORIGINAL SCREENPLAY]

ITALY
DIAMOND FILM AWARDS JUL 2019
[WINNER (NARRATIVE
FEATURE FILM)]

...and more!

For more information, visit **www.immortal-hero.com**

THE REAL EXORCIST

55 Awards from 8 Countries!

STORY Tokyo —the most mystical city in the world where you find
spiritual spots in the most unexpected places. Sayuri works as a part time
waitress at a small coffee shop "Extra" where regular customers enjoy
the authentic coffee that the owner brews. Meanwhile, Sayuri uses her
supernatural powers to help those who are troubled by spiritual phenomena
one after another. Through her special consultations, she touches the hearts
of the people and helps them by showing the truths of the invisible world.

USA
GOLD REMI AWARD
53rd WorldFest Houston
International Film Festival 2020

MONACO
BEST FEATURE FILM
17th Angel Film Awards
2020
Monaco International Film Festival

BEST FEMALE ACTOR
17th Angel Film Awards
2020
Monaco International Film Festival

NIGERIA
BEST FEATURE FILM
EKO International Film Festival
2020

BEST FEMALE SUPPORTING ACTOR
17th Angel Film Awards
2020
Monaco International Film Festival

BEST SUPPORTING ACTRESS
EKO International Film Festival
2020

BEST VISUAL EFFECTS
17th Angel Film Awards
2020
Monaco International Film Festival

...and more!

For more information, visit **www.realexorcistmovie.com**

ABOUT IRH PRESS USA

IRH Press USA Inc. was founded in 2013 as an affiliated firm of IRH Press Co., Ltd. Based in New York, the press publishes books in various categories including spirituality, religion, and self-improvement and publishes books by Ryuho Okawa, the author of over 100 million books sold worldwide. For more information, visit *okawabooks.com*.

Follow us on:

Facebook: Okawa Books   **Twitter**: Okawa Books

Goodreads: Ryuho Okawa   **Instagram**: OkawaBooks

Pinterest: Okawa Books

RYUHO OKAWA'S LAWS SERIES

The Laws Series is an annual volume of books that are mainly comprised of Ryuho Okawa's lectures on various topics that highlight principles and guidelines for the activities of Happy Science every year. *The Laws of the Sun*, the first publication of the Laws Series, ranked in the annual best-selling list in Japan. Since then, all of the Laws Series' titles have ranked in the annual best-selling list for more than two decades, setting socio-cultural trends in Japan and around the world.

THE TRILOGY

The first three volumes of the Laws Series, *The Laws of the Sun*, *The Golden Laws*, and *The Nine Dimensions* make a trilogy that completes the basic framework of the teachings of God's Truths. *The Laws of the Sun* discusses the structure of God's Laws, *The Golden Laws* expounds on the doctrine of time, and *The Nine Dimensions* reveals the nature of space.

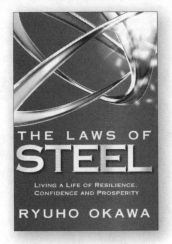

The 26th Laws Series

THE LAWS OF STEEL

LIVING A LIFE OF RESILIENCE, CONFIDENCE AND PROSPERITY

Paperback • 256 pages • $16.95
ISBN: 978-1-942125-65-5

This book is a compilation of six lectures that Ryuho Okawa gave in 2018 and 2019, each containing passionate messages for us to open a brighter future. This powerful and inspiring book will not only show us the ways to achieve true happiness and prosperity, but also the ways to solve many global issues we now face. It presents us with wisdom that is based on a spiritual perspective, and a new design for our future society. Through this book, we can overcome differences in values and create a peaceful world, thereby ushering in a Golden Age.

Chapter list

1 The Mindset to Invite Prosperity

2 The Law of Cause and Effect

3 Fulfilling *Noblesse Oblige*

4 Be Confident in Your Life

5 A Savior's Wish

6 The Power to Make Miracles

*For a complete list of books, visit **okawabooks.com***

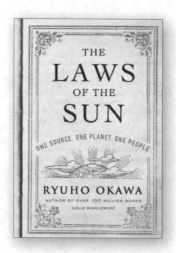

THE LAWS OF THE SUN
ONE SOURCE, ONE PLANET, ONE PEOPLE

Paperback • 288 pages • $15.95
ISBN: 978-1-942125-43-3

IMAGINE IF YOU COULD ASK GOD why He created this world and what spiritual laws He used to shape us—and everything around us. If we could understand His designs and intentions, we could discover what our goals in life should be and whether our actions move us closer to those goals or farther away.

At a young age, a spiritual calling prompted Ryuho Okawa to outline what he innately understood to be universal truths for all humankind. In *The Laws of the Sun*, Okawa outlines these laws of the universe and provides a road map for living one's life with greater purpose and meaning.

In this powerful book, Ryuho Okawa reveals the transcendent nature of consciousness and the secrets of our multidimensional universe and our place in it. By understanding the different stages of love and following the Buddhist Eightfold Path, he believes we can speed up our eternal process of development. *The Laws of the Sun* shows the way to realize true happiness—a happiness that continues from this world through the other.

*For a complete list of books, visit **okawabooks.com***

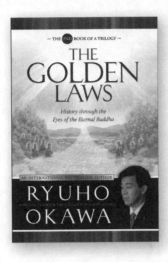

THE GOLDEN LAWS
HISTORY THROUGH THE EYES OF THE ETERNAL BUDDHA

Paperback • 201 pages • $14.95
ISBN: 978-1-941779-81-1

Throughout history, Great Guiding Spirits of Light have been present on Earth in both the East and the West at crucial points in human history to further our spiritual development. *The Golden Laws* reveals how Divine Plan has been unfolding on Earth, and outlines 5,000 years of the secret history of humankind. Once we understand the true course of history, through past, present and into the future, we cannot help but become aware of the significance of our spiritual mission in the present age.

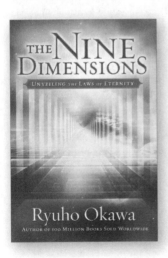

THE NINE DIMENSIONS
UNVEILING THE LAWS OF ETERNITY

Paperback • 168 pages • $15.95
ISBN: 978-0-982698-56-3

This book is a window into the mind of our loving God, who designed this world and the vast, wondrous world of our afterlife as a school with many levels through which our souls learn and grow. When the religions and cultures of the world discover the truth of their common spiritual origin, they will be inspired to accept their differences, come together under faith in God, and build an era of harmony and peaceful progress on Earth.

*For a complete list of books, visit **okawabooks.com***

THE REAL EXORCIST

ATTAIN WISDOM TO CONQUER EVIL

Paperback • 208 pages • $16.95
ISBN:978-1-942125-67-9

This is a profound spiritual text backed by the author's nearly 40 years of real-life experience with spiritual phenomena. In it, Okawa teaches how we may discern and overcome our negative tendencies, by acquiring the right knowledge, mindset and lifestyle.

THE NEW RESURRECTION

MY MIRACULOUS STORY OF OVERCOMING ILLNESS AND DEATH

Hardcover • 224 pages • $19.95
ISBN: 978-1-942125-64-8

The New Resurrection is an autobiographical account of an astonishing miracle experienced by author Ryuho Okawa in 2004. This event was adapted into the feature-length film *Immortal Hero*, released in Japan, the United States and Canada during the Fall of 2019. Today, Okawa lives each day with the readiness to die for the Truth and has dedicated his life to selflessly guiding faith seekers towards spiritual development and happiness. The appendix showcases a myriad of accomplishments by Okawa, chronicled after his miraculous resurrection.

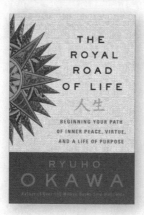

THE ROYAL ROAD OF LIFE

BEGINNING YOUR PATH OF INNER PEACE, VIRTUE, AND A LIFE OF PURPOSE

Paperback • 224 pages • $16.95
ISBN: 978-1-942125-53-2

With over 30 years of lectures and teachings spanning diverse topics of faith, self-growth, leadership (and more), Ryuho Okawa presents the profound eastern wisdom that he has cultivated on his approach to life. *The Royal Road of Life* illuminates a path to becoming a person of virtue, whose character and depth will move and inspire others towards the same meaningful destination.

---

*For a complete list of books, visit **okawabooks.com***

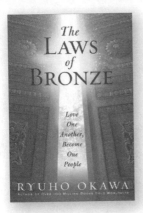

THE LAWS OF BRONZE

LOVE ONE ANOTHER, BECOME ONE PEOPLE

Paperback • 224 pages • $15.95
ISBN: 978-1-942125-50-1

With the advancement of science and technology leading to longer life-span, many people are seeking out a way to lead a meaningful life with purpose and direction. This book will show people from all walks of life that they can solve their problems in life both on an individual level and on a global scale by finding faith and practicing love. When all of us in this planet discover our common spiritual origin revealed in this book, we can truly love one another and become one people on Earth.

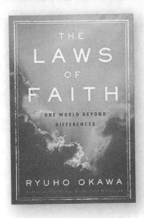

THE LAWS OF FAITH

ONE WORLD BEYOND DIFFERENCES

Paperback • 208 pages • $15.95
ISBN: 978-1-942125-34-1

Ryuho Okawa preaches at the core of a new universal religion from various angles while integrating logical and spiritual viewpoints in mind with current world situations. This book offers us the key to accept diversities beyond differences in ethnicity, religion, race, gender, descent, and so on, harmonize the individuals and nations and create a world filled with peace and prosperity.

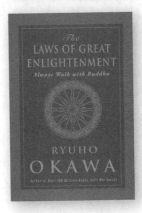

THE LAWS OF GREAT ENLIGHTENMENT

ALWAYS WALK WITH BUDDHA

Paperback • 232 pages • $17.95
ISBN: 978-1-942125-62-4

Constant self-blame for mistakes, setbacks, or failures and feelings of unforgivingness toward others are hard to overcome. Through the power of enlightenment we can learn to forgive ourselves and others, overcome life's problems, and courageously create a brighter future ourselves. *The Laws of Great Enlightenment* addresses the core problems of life that people often struggle with and offers advice on how to overcome them based on spiritual truths.

*For a complete list of books, visit **okawabooks.com***

LOVE, NURTURE, AND FORGIVE
A Handbook to Add a New Richness to Your Life

LOVE FOR THE FUTURE
Building One World of Freedom and Democracy Under God's Truth

THE LAWS OF INVINCIBLE LEADERSHIP
An Empowering Guide for Continuous and
Lasting Success in Business and in Life

WORRY-FREE LIVING
Let Go of Stress and Live in Peace and Happiness

THE CHALLENGE OF THE MIND
An Essential Guide to Buddha's Teachings:
Zen, Karma, and Enlightenment

THE STRONG MIND
The Art of Building the Inner Strength to Overcome Life's Difficulties

THE STARTING POINT OF HAPPINESS
An Inspiring Guide to Positive Living with Faith, Love, and Courage

THINK BIG!
Be Positive and Be Brave to Achieve Your Dreams

THE ESSENCE OF BUDDHA
The Path to Enlightenment

THE MIRACLE OF MEDITATION
Opening Your Life to Peace, Joy, and the Power Within

For a complete list of books, visit **okawabooks.com**